NEW SKILLS
FOR FRAZZLED
PARENTS

The Instruction Manual that Should Have Come with Your Child

Daniel G. Amen, M.D.
Neuroscientist & Child Psychiatrist

D1286711

MindWorks Press
4019 Westerly Place, Suite #100
Newport Beach, CA 92660
(949) 266-3730

ISBN 1-886554-02-1
Manufactured in the United States of America
9 8 7 6

Other Books by Dr. Amen

CHANGE YOUR BRAIN, CHANGE YOUR LIFE

WINDOWS INTO THE A.D.D. MIND:
Understanding and Treating Attention Deficit Disorder
Childhood Through Adulthood

COACHING YOURSELF TO SUCCESS
A Step-by-Step Guide For Identifying and Achieving Your Goals

FIRESTORMS IN THE BRAIN
An Inside Look At Violence

HEALING THE CHAOS WITHIN
The Interaction Between A.D.D., Alcoholism
and Growing Up In an Alcoholic Home

MINDCOACH FOR KIDS
Teaching Kids and Teens To Think Positive and Feel Good

WOULD YOU GIVE TWO MINUTES A DAY
FOR A LIFETIME OF LOVE?

TEN STEPS TO BUILDING VALUES WITHIN CHILDREN

A TEENAGER'S GUIDE TO A.D.D.

Confidentiality is essential to psychiatric practice. All case descriptions in this book, therefore, have been altered to preserve the anonymity of my patients without distorting the essentials of their stories.

The information offered in this book is not intended to be a substitute for the advice and counsel of your personal physician. Consult with your physician before making any medical changes.

Dedication

To Antony
Breanne
Kaitlyn

You have given me all my gray hairs and
taught me everything I know
about being a real parent.
I know madness and joy because of you.
I would never change a second of our time!

The best parents are..................

Firm

Kind

Bonded

Consistent

Positive

Attentive

Thoughtful

Authoritative

Affectionate

TABLE OF CONTENTS

Introduction

"There are times when parenthood seems like nothing more than feeding the hand that bites you."   -- Peter De Vries

"Insanity is hereditary. You get it from your kids."
                                                    -- Sam Levinson

"Only the sinner has the right to preach." -- Christopher Morley

Never trust a child psychiatrist who doesn't have kids! In order to teach you about effectively raising kids a professional must have at least some sense of what you're going through as a parent. He (or she), at some point, must have experienced the same exhilaration, joy, frustration and fear that comes with being a parent. It is even helpful if your professional has said to himself, "This is more than I can do. I want to run away from home." Now, of course, if the professional ran away from home because he couldn't deal with his kids you should find someone else!

I have three children, (at the time of this writing) a twenty-two year old son, a sixteen year old daughter and an eleven year old daughter. None of my kids are perfect. Two of my children have been diagnosed with Attention Deficit Disorder (by professionals other than myself). At times they have been very difficult for my wife and I to parent. Using the techniques in this course have been invaluable to us! They have helped us survive the difficult stages of childhood and helped us give our children a personal sense of responsibility, motivation, self esteem and interpersonal connectedness which helps them be successful day-to-day.

Parenting a child is one of the most important responsibilities any of us ever undertake. Yet, it does not require any special training or any prior experience. I've heard it said that parents make most of their mistakes with the first child, overcompensate with the second child, and finally get it right with the third child. Being a third child myself I like to think that my parents learned from their mistakes just in time. Today, however, since most families have 2 children or less there's no time to lose.

Parenting any child is a challenge and requires solid skills. Parenting difficult children requires "superior" parenting skills if you are going to be really helpful to them. This program is designed to give you the best parenting skills in a fun and practical way that will give you clear, quick, and lasting results. I have taught this parenting course for the past 12 years and I find that it is by far one of the most effective things I do to help kids.

Parents are generally the most important people in a child's life. Unfortunately, parents often underestimate their own influence in raising children and teenagers. Their busy lives often prevent them from focusing their energy on raising healthy kids. Many parents delegate the "important stuff" (such as teaching values or teaching about sex and drugs) to churches and schools. It is critical for parents take back their role of being the primary teacher in a child's life and use their power in a way that positively directs a child's life.

If you do the exercises in the workbook this course will help you:

* set clear goals for yourself as a parent and for the child

* understand why children struggle

* understand why parents struggle

* help you establish the best "interactive fit" between you and your child

* understand the stepping stones of normal development

* dramatically improve the quality of your relationship with your child

* establish clear family rules and values

* give you rules for giving effective commands

* help you avoid parenting traps

* help you think clearly and logically in dealing with your child

* be very reinforcing when your child's behavior is pleasing to you

* be able to give clear, unemotional consequences when your child's behavior is out of line

* get your child to mind you the first time you say something (Yes, I said the first time!)

* effectively manage public misbehavior

* provide solid supervision

* give your child appropriate choices

Two words emphasized over and over in this course will be firm and kind. **FIRM** and **KIND** summarize the characteristics of good parenting.

New Skills For Frazzled Parents is a comprehensive program that will shape parent-child interactions in a proactive, positive way. The best endorsement for this course came from an Oakland Police Officer. His wife brought their ten-year-old son Tim to see me on the advice of the school psychologist. Tim was having problems in school. He got into fights on the playground, he refused to do his homework, and he seemed angry and depressed. Tim's father wanted nothing to do with seeing a shrink. "He just needs a good spanking," was a common phrase from the father. At my insistence, the father reluctantly came to the first appointment. After the evaluation it was clear to me that one of Tim's major problems was a lack of closeness to his father. Tim felt he could never please his father and that his father thought he was just a "screw up." Since this family lived over an hour from my clinic and could not come regularly for appointments I persuaded the father to listen to the set of parenting tapes in this program. At their first follow-up appointment a month later things in this family dramatically changed. Rather than blaming Tim for the problems he had, the father took an active role in helping Tim. He spent "special time" with Tim (a major component of this course), learned how to use praise, and took a problem solving approach to Tim's struggles. After several months the father wrote me a letter saying, "This course changed my whole relationship with my son. I went from being angry, ineffective and critical to loving, present, and firm. For the first time in many years I feel joy when I'm around my son instead of frustration." Later he told me, "I'm so grateful you helped me be effective with my son. Unknowingly, I was setting him up for disaster. So many of the kids we pick up on the street for criminal behavior have problems with their parents. Tim was a lot more vulnerable when we were not close."

I know this course works. I believe this course (or one like it) should be required before people have children. There is too much at stake if parents do a poor job. I am very serious when I tell you that this course may change your child's life, and for that matter, the lives of your grandchildren and their children. Parenting is a skill we learn mostly from our parents. If you do it right, your children are more likely to do a good job with their own children, and on and on. Do it wrong and generational problems are likely to follow. Do all of the exercises in the book, and if desired watch and listen to the tapes that are companions to the book. It is the fastest way to more peace and harmony at home.

Chapter One

ESTABLISHING TOTAL FOCUS AS A PARENT

The most important step in the parenting process is goal setting. It is critical, as a parent or parents, to know clearly what you are trying to accomplish. What is the goal? What are you trying to achieve by your day-to-day interactions with your child? With clear goals you act in a way that is proactive and positive, consistent with your goals. Without a clear vision of what you want for your child you become reactive, ineffective and easily frustrated. Knowing what you want for yourself as a parent and for your child is critical to acting in a way to make it happen. Ultimately, it is our goals and our visions that determine our behavior. This is especially important in parenting. Being clear with what you are trying to achieve with your child will take your behavior out of the realm of an unconscious repetition of the past and focus your actions into behaviors that move you and your child in a positive direction.

I am a firm believer that you have to look at your goals EVERYDAY. Looking at them everyday takes them out of the realm of wishful thinking and places them in the realm of everyday behavior. If you only look at your goals infrequently they have a fate similar to most New Year's Resolutions -- disappointment.

Here is the set of "my" own parenting goals. I have them in the top drawer of my desk at work. My wife also has a set, as we did these together (a process I strongly recommend). We both start the day looking at these goals, along with other personal goals. Starting the day with these goals in mind helps us to keep our behavior consistent with what we want. My bet is that you are probably like me: raising effective children is at the top of your priority list. You are also probably like me in that you can get too busy and not pay close enough attention to the things in your life that really matter. That is why I have developed these goals for myself and feel it is essential to look at them on a daily basis. These goals help to keep me on task.

If you like my goals, copy them and look at them everyday. If you wish, revise them to fit your own goals and desires for your children, adding your own special touches. Then put them up where you can see them everyday. Everyday ask yourself, "Is my behavior getting me what I want for myself as a parent and what I want for my child?"

Goals For Parents

As a parent -- THE OVERALL GOAL IS BE A COMPETENT, POSITIVE FORCE IN THE CHILD'S LIFE

1. BE INVOLVED -- I want to be there for my children, so I will ensure that I have enough time for them.

2. BE OPEN -- I will talk with them in such a way that will help them talk to me when they need to.

3. BE FIRM/SET LIMITS -- I will provide appropriate supervision and limits until they develop their own moral/internal controls.

4. BE TOGETHER -- Whether married or divorced, it is best for our children when we agree and support each other in the process.

5. BE KIND -- I will raise my children in such a way so that they will want to come see me after they leave home. Being a parent is also a selfish job.

6. BE FUN -- I will joke, clown and play with my kids. Having fun is essential to physical and emotional health.

Goals For Children

For children -- THE OVERALL GOAL IS TO ENHANCE DEVELOPMENT

1. BE RELATIONAL -- We live in a relational world. It is imperative that I teach my children how to get along with others.

2. BE RESPONSIBLE -- My children need to believe and act as if they have some control over their own life. That their problems are not always someone else's fault. Otherwise, they act like victims.

3. BE INDEPENDENT -- I will allow my children to have some choices over their own lives so that they will be able to make good decisions on their own.

4. BE SELF-CONFIDENT -- I will encourage my children to be involved with different activities where they will feel a sense of competence. Self-confidence often comes from our ability to be able to master tasks and sports.

5. BE SELF-ACCEPTING -- I will notice more positive than negative in my children to teach them to be able to accept themselves.

6. BE ADAPTABLE -- I will expose my children to different situations so that they will be flexible enough to deal with the various stresses that will come their way.

7. BE EMOTIONALLY FREE -- I will allow my children the ability to express themselves in an accepting environment. I will also seek help for my children if they show prolonged symptoms of emotional trouble.

8. BE FUN -- I will teach my child how to have fun and how to laugh.

Chapter Two

TEACH YOUR CHILDREN TO SET GOALS

In order for children to be successful in the world it is critical we teach them to set their own goals. As with adults, when children know what they want they are more likely to match their behavior to get it. I have many of my patients, whether they are 6 or 75 years old, do an exercise called the One Page Miracle, which I will share with you shortly.

Goal setting is a function of the frontal lobes of the brain, the most evolved part of the human brain. In order for this part of our brain to be as effective as possible it's important to know what you want, to know what is important to you. Being goal-directed helps keep our behavior on track.

When I ask children about their goals many of them look at me with blank stares or they mutter something about being a fireman or doctor when they grow up. Goal setting is not for some far off dream. It is for now and it is very specific. Teaching children to make short and long-term goals and focus on them daily will make a positive difference.

The ONE PAGE MIRACLE (OPM) is an exercise I developed over 10 years ago to help children, teens, and adults be effective in their day-to-day lives. In studying successful kids and adults I found that they had two things in common: a sense of personal responsibility, and clear goals. The exercise is still in a file titled "GOALS" on my computer. It was named The ONE PAGE MIRACLE after I saw how it changed people's lives. It is an exercise that will help guide nearly all of your child's thoughts, words and actions. I've seen this exercise quickly focus and change many people.

Here are the directions to help your child develop their own OPM. Parents you need to do this with the child (perhaps even do one of your own). Act like your child's secretary. Take one sheet of paper and clearly write out your major goals. Use the following main headings: Relationships, School/Work, and Myself. Under Relationships write the subheadings of parents, siblings and friends. Under School/Work write current and future school and work goals. Under Myself write out body, feelings, faith, and hobbies.

Next to each subheading clearly write out what's important to the child in that area; write what he wants, not what he doesn't want. Initially get input from the child. If she is having a hard time thinking of something use the example below or coach them with suggestions. Be positive and write in the first person. Both the parent and child can keep a copy with them for several days so that it can be worked on over time. After you finish with the initial draft (you'll frequently want to update it), place this piece of paper where you and the child can see it everyday, such as on your refrigerator, by your child's bed or on the bathroom mirror. That way, everyday your child can focus his eyes on what's important to him. This makes it easier to match his behavior to what he wants. His life will become more conscious and he will spend his energy on goals that are important to him.

I separate the areas of relationships, school/work, and myself in order to encourage a balanced approach to life. Burnout occurs when lives become unbalanced and over-extended in one area while ignoring another.

Here is an actual example from one of my patient's, nine year old Jenny, who was in third grade and had an older brother. She came to see me for problems with anxiety. After you look at the example fill out the OPM with your child. Then put it up where you and the child can see and read it everyday. It is a great idea to start the day off by reading the OPM to get focused for the day.

Jenny's
ONE PAGE MIRACLE
What Do I Want for My Life?

RELATIONSHIPS

Parents: I want to have a kind, loving relationship with my mom and dad. I want them to trust me and be proud of me.

Siblings: I realize that my brother will always be my family. Even though we may fight sometimes, I will treat him the way that I would want him to treat me.

Friends: It is important to have friends. I will treat other people with kindness and respect. I will make new friends with kids who have the same kinds of goals I have.

SCHOOL/WORK

School is for me. It is to help me be the best person I can be. I give school my best effort everyday. I want to learn and become a smart person.

Teacher: My teachers are there to help me. I will treat them with respect and kindness.

Work: When I have work to do, either around the house or at a job someday, I will do my best and feel proud of my effort. I will help around the house and do my chores with a good attitude. I know I need to help my family and do my part.

MYSELF

1. To be healthy
2. To take care of my body
3. To feel good, happy
4. To live in a way that makes me feel proud
5. To live close to God and be the kind of person He would want me to be

Name:_____
ONE PAGE MIRACLE
What Do I Want for My Life?

RELATIONSHIPS

Parents:

_____
_____

Siblings:

_____
_____

Friends:

_____
_____

SCHOOL/WORK

_____
_____

Teacher:_____

Work:_____
_____

MYSELF

Body:_____

Mind:_____

Spirit:_____

Interests/Hobbies:_____

Teach your kids to be focused on what's important to them. It'll make your job as a parent easier and more effective.

Chapter Three

FOUR STYLES OF PARENTING

Parenting is often viewed along two lines:

from loving to hostile and

from firm to permissive.

When we graph these lines together we come up with 4 parenting styles.

	Loving ———————— Hostile	
Firm	LF Loving and Firm	HF Hostile and Firm
Permissive	LP Loving and Permissive	HP Hostile and Permissive

Here is a brief description of the four parenting styles:

Hostile and Permissive (HP): HP parents are those parents who do not care. They are angry people and often detached from their child. There is a lack of bonding, caring, and adequate supervision. When I described this type of parent in one of my parenting classes a police officer gave the following example of the HP parent: "I knew a father who gave his 15 year old son a $100 bill and told him that he didn't want to see his face all weekend long."

Loving and Permissive (LP): This parenting style describes those parents who are sweet and kind to their children and give them anything they want. They hate to frustrate their children at all and give in to their every whim. The best example of this parenting style is the pretty six year old girl with blonde ringlets who is in the middle of a party screaming to get her way as her parents are scrambling to give her what she wants.

Hostile and Firm (HF): This is the military "first sergeant" type. I was an army psychiatrist for 7 years and knew many HF parents (although the military had all three other groups as well). HF parents want it done their way and they get their child's compliance through anger, intimidation, and fear. A typical statement might be, "You do it when I say it, how I say it, without any questions. I hope you got it!"

Loving and Firm (LF): These parents demand respect and believe that their children need to mind the first time. They are also reinforcing, warm, positive and uplifting to the children. They know how to give options and choices, yet they have high expectations for good behavior. The best words to describe this group is FIRM and KIND.

Which "parenting style" do you think has the most problems with their children?

_____

Which "parenting style" do you think has the next worst problems with their children?

_____

Which "parenting style" do you think has the fewest problems with their children?

_____

The kids who have the most problems come from HP parents. By being hostile and permissive there is very little bonding between the parents and child and little to no direction. That is a deadly combination. Often these children have severe psychiatric problems or significant trouble with the law. Without good bonding between a parent and a child, the child grows up not caring about others and can hurt others without it affecting their conscience. Without clear direction in life children flounder and often gravitate toward the lowest peer group.

Many people think that the next group with the worst problems are from the "first sergeant" HF group. Research, however, does not bear that out. The LP group of kids has more problems. Uniformly, permissiveness is not helpful for children. Even though these children get love and acceptance, they get no direction and they get their way with their parents. When you are use to getting your way with a tantrum you continue that behavior at school and with your peer group. Teachers and peers do not like demanding kids who use tantrums or whining to get their way.

Clearly, the HF parent is not a good role model. Hostile and controlling parents tend to breed children who are oppositional, anxious and moody. Yet, given a choice between being firm or being permissive it is probably more helpful for the child to lean toward the firm side.

As you've guessed, the kids who do best are those whose parents fit into the LF group. Kids need clear direction and clear lines of authority. They also need an atmosphere of love and kindness. Giving clear direction and being able to back it up is important. It teaches kids a sense of authority and self-discipline, which are very important concepts if the child is going to be successful now and in the future.

Chapter Four

STEPPING STONES OF NORMAL DEVELOPMENT

Another prerequisite to parenting difficult kids is to understand normal child development. This will allow parents to know when things are on track and when there is a problem. Having general information about development also helps us have reasonable expectations for our children.

Major Points to Remember:

1. Children do not think like adults.

2. Children go through well-established stages of development. They are not born with adult thoughts or behaviors.

3. Children often do not know why they do certain things. They are driven by internal factors that motivate them to move along developmental stages. Sometimes when they experience traumatic events (such as divorce of their parents, death of a parent or sibling, physical or sexual abuse) they remain stuck at an earlier stage. We call this developmental arrest.

4. Children most often express their needs and anxieties through their behavior.

Here are some of the major milestones and tasks of development.

Infants: birth to 18 months

- completely dependent

- unable to delay wants or needs

- think that they and their mother are much the same person

- learn mostly through their senses

Toddlers: 18 months to 3 years

- begin to realize that they are separate, independent people and begin to exert independence by saying "NO" and "I want to do it myself."

- new independence often frightens them, so they often have "FEARS" and tend to be more clinging.

- they develop a sense of confidence if they are allowed to exert independent behavior (under adequate supervision) versus a sense of self-consciousness if they are overcontrolled.

Preschoolers: 3 to 6 years

- show initiative and curiosity -- they ask many questions

- highly imaginative -- often have imaginary friends, some trouble separating reality from fantasy

- think magically -- think that their thoughts have power and that they are responsible for everything around them, a trait that sometimes leads to lifelong guilt. When something good happens they feel pride. When something bad happens during this stage (divorce, death of a sibling, etc.) they often feel tremendous guilt, thinking somehow it was their fault.

- engage in competition to replace parent of same sex. Sometimes this is very mild, sometimes it is quite severe.

Early School Age: 6 to 11 years

- develops friendships and ties outside home (brownies, soccer, etc.)

- identifies with parent of same sex

- attention span dramatically increases

- thinks more in literal terms, things are often black or white

- needs supervision, rules and structure to feel comfortable

Pre-teen and Early Teenagers: 11 to 14 years

- begin to move toward more independent thinking

- struggle with sense of identity

- close friendships gain increasing importance, more heavily influenced by peer group

- realize parents aren't perfect and identify their faults for them

- shyness about their body

- rule and limit testing

Mid Teenagers: 14 to 17

- move toward further independence, complain parents interfere with this or that and that they are overly protective

- extremely concerned about physical appearance

- strong emphasis on peer group, withdraw emotions from parents in an effort to be able to separate from them in a short while

- more interest in specific careers

- frequently changing relationships

Late Teenagers: 17 to 19

- have a firmer identity

- more ability to delay needs and wants, can work for things down the road

- better able to anticipate consequences to actions

- higher level of concern for the future

- greater concern for others, more stable relationships

These are just broad guidelines and every child goes through development at their own pace. Difficult children are often "stuck" or delayed in their development. Understanding these "stepping stones" of development will help you know where your child or teenager is emotionally.

Chapter Five

WHY CHILDREN STRUGGLE

There are many reasons children misbehave. It is important to try to understand, because if you know the reasons they are having trouble with their behavior you're more likely to use the right interventions. Here are some common reasons:

ATTENTION

When a child gets little positive attention they will seek negative attention. Any attention is better than no attention at all. Attention from parents is critical to the development of a child's sense of themselves and their self-esteem. Without significant attention from parents they flounder.

CONTROL

Some children misbehave as a way to rule the nest. When parents are too controlling or they allow the child to be too manipulative power issues come into play. Overcontrolling parents breed oppositional behavior in kids. At the same time, if you are a wimp and the child can get his or her way by whining, yelling or screaming you give them power they are more than willing to take. When in doubt, firm and kind is the rule to follow.

TO GET EVEN

When a child is hurt or angered by parents they may misbehave as a way to get back at them. Little do they realize that they are hurting themselves in the process.

HELPLESSNESS

Some kids misbehave as a way to get out of doing things. If they can appear helpless (to clean their room or do the dishes) and the parent buys in to it, the helplessness gives them a powerful tool to escape work. Try to never allow a child to get out of doing their responsibilities through feigning helplessness.

LACK OF GOOD TEACHING

Some kids are never taught to behave in an acceptable way. Their parents have the idea that their child is born knowing how to be socially appropriate and they abdicate their parental role as teacher. Children are not born knowing the ropes of life like some animal species. They need to be taught by loving, present parents.

If any of the above is an issue for your child this course will be of tremendous value for you.

Sometimes children or teens misbehave because of other reasons, such as underlying emotional or neurological problems (ADD, depression, anxiety, learning disabilities, etc.)

Between 10-20% of kids have an emotional or learning problem that interferes with their ability to manage their behavior. It is very common for parents who take my course to have one of these children. Clearly, they are more difficult to parent. For that reason I will go into depth on this issue. For those parents whose children do not have any of these problems it is a good time to light candles at church and be thankful (or be thankful in any way that best fits).

Here's an example of a teenager with an emotional problem:

Fifteen-year-old Christine just got her progress report: 1 C-, 3 Ds and 2 Fs. This was the second year in a row this bright girl was failing in school for no apparent reason. The parents were at their wits end. They tried offering her help, giving her incentives, yelling and grounding her, but nothing worked. Christine was withdrawn, without motivation, irritable and had trouble sleeping. She occasionally thought of suicide, but didn't have the energy to follow through on her thoughts. When her parents brought her in for an evaluation it was clear to me that Christine was clinically depressed. She also had a grandfather who was an alcoholic and an aunt who had been hospitalized for depression. Depression, along with other mental or brain disorders, often goes unnoticed in children and teenagers, rather these kids get labeled as lazy or uninterested.
Whenever a child or teen goes through significant problems with their family, friends or schoolwork it is important to evaluate what may be the problem.

Unfortunately, many parents become frustrated or angry with their child rather than objectively evaluating the situation. Kids who are having trouble need more time and understanding from their parents, *not hostility or blame.* Here are several clinical possibilities that may explain difficult behavior or school failure in kids or teens.

Depression is a common emotional problem in children and teenagers. It is characterized by:

- prolonged periods of sadness,
- irritability,
- poor concentration and memory,
- loss of motivation or interest,
- marked increase or decrease in sleep,
- marked decreased or increased appetite,
- low energy,
- feelings of helplessness, hopelessness or worthlessness,
- a tendency to only think negative thoughts, and
- suicidal thoughts (often not expressed to anyone).

Children and teens also suffer from anxiety, although this problem is usually overlooked or discounted. Common symptoms include:

- periods of nervousness,
- increased tension,
- emotional reactivity,
- physical stress symptoms such as headaches or stomach aches,
- unreasonable fears,
- a tendency to predict bad things,
- sleep or appetite problems,
- restlessness, and
- periods of panic.

Attention deficit disorders (ADD) are also often overlooked in children and teens and may cause lifelong problems when it is overlooked or misdiagnosed. Many people still think that ADD is just a fad or something that kids outgrow. Yet, when ADD is left untreated it causes serious life problems. For example:

O 35% of people with ADD never finish high school

O 43% of boys with ADD will be arrested for a felony by the time they're 16

O 52% of people with ADD will have drug or alcohol problems

O 75% of people with ADD have relationship problems as children and adults

Many people think that ADD is just an excuse for poor grades or bad behavior. Teachers and parents often tell kids with ADD that if only they would try harder they'd do better. Unfortunately, that is not true. In fact, the harder people with ADD try, the worse it gets. Attention Deficit Disorder (ADD) is the most common learning problem among children, teens and adults. It affects more than 17 million Americans.

There are two major types of ADD.

ADHD, or ADD with hyperactivity (classic ADD)
ADD, without hyperactivity (couch potatoes)

At my clinic we have identified four additional types of this disorder. They also occur in various combinations:

ADD, overfocused (tend to get stuck)
ADD, depressive (negative and irritable)
ADD, violent, explosive (dark thoughts)
ADD, ring of fire (angry, oppositional and cyclic mood changes)

Here are the major symptoms for the subtypes of ADD. Use the checklists to see if any apply to your children or teens. I have included the part of the brain suspected to be involved with each subtype in parentheses.

CRITERIA FOR AD/HD
Attention-Deficit/Hyperactivity Disorder from DSM-IV
(Prefrontal Cortex System)

Either (1) or (2) needed for diagnosis

(1) six (or more) of the following symptoms of inattention have persisted for at least six months to a degree that is maladaptive and inconsistent with developmental level:

Inattention
____ 1. often fails to give close attention to details or makes careless mistakes in schoolwork, work, or other activities
____ 2. often has difficulty sustaining attention in tasks or play activities
____ 3. often does not seem to listen when spoken to directly
____ 4. often does not follow through on instructions and fails to finish schoolwork, chores, or duties in the workplace (not due to oppositional behavior or failure to understand instructions)
____ 5. often has difficulty organizing tasks and activities
____ 6. often avoids, dislikes, or is reluctant to engage in tasks that require sustained mental effort (such as schoolwork or homework)
____ 7. often loses things necessary for tasks or activities (e.g., toys, school assignments, pencils, books, or tools)
____ 8. is often easily distracted by extraneous stimuli
____ 9. is often forgetful in daily activities

(2) six (or more) of the following symptoms of hyperactivity-impulsivity have persisted for at least six months to a degree that is maladaptive and inconsistent with developmental level:

Hyperactivity
____ 1. often fidgets with hands or feet or squirms in seat
____ 2. often leaves seat in classroom or in other situations in which remaining seated is expected
____ 3. often runs about or climbs excessively in situations in which it is inappropriate (in adolescents or adults, may be limited to subjective feelings of restlessness)
____ 4. often has difficulty playing or engaging in leisure activities quietly
____ 5. is often "on the go" or often acts as if "driven by a motor"
____ 6. often talks excessively

Impulsivity

   ___ 7. often blurts out answers before questions have been completed

   ___ 8. often has difficulty awaiting turn

   ___ 9. often interrupts or intrudes on others (e.g., butts into conversations or games)

The onset of at least some symptoms must be before age seven and they must have lasted at least for six months. In order to make the diagnosis, some impairment from the symptoms is present in two or more settings (e.g., school [or work] and at home). There must also be clear evidence of clinically significant impairment in social, academic, or occupational functioning. The severity of the disorder is rated as mild, moderate or severe.

Based on DSM-IV criteria, there can be three subtypes:

AD/HD, combined type,
> if both criterion for 1 and 2 are met

AD/HD, predominantly inattentive type,
> if criterion 1 is met but criterion 2 is not

AD/HD, predominantly hyperactive-impulsive type,
> if criterion 2 is met but criterion 1 is not

The boys with AD/HD combined or predominantly hyperactive-impulsive type are often identified early in life. The level of hyperactivity, restlessness and impulsivity causes them to stand out from others. AD/HD predominantly inattentive type girls, on the other hand, may be ignored because they get labeled as "social butterflies." Even as we near the next century, societal expectations are different for girls than they are for boys.

Brain studies of patients with classic AD/HD reveal a decrease in brain activity in the frontal lobes of the brain in response to an intellectual challenge. The harder these people try to concentrate, the worse it gets. Having less activity in the front part of the brain is a very uncomfortable state of mind. Due to this many of these kids unconsciously become very stimulation seeking. Increased activity level, restlessness and humming are common ways these kids try to stimulate themselves. Another way these kids try to turn their brains on is by causing turmoil. If they can get their parents to yell at them or somehow cause increased turmoil at home or in the classroom that might cause increased activity in their frontal lobes and make them feel more tuned in. Again, this is not a conscious phenomenon. These children do not know that they are doing this to become turned on. It seems many of these kids become addicted to the turmoil. They repeatedly get others upset with them even though there is no benefit to their behavior.

The parents of these children commonly report that they are experts at getting them upset. One mother told me that when she wakes up in the morning she promises herself that she won't yell or get upset with her 8 year old son. Yet, invariably by the time he is off for school there have been at least three fights and both of them feel terrible. When I explained the child's unconscious need for stimulation to the mother she stopped yelling at him. When parents stop providing the negative stimulation (yelling, spanking, lecturing, etc.) these children decrease the negative behaviors. Whenever you feel like screaming at one of these kids talk as softly as you can. At least in that way you're breaking their addiction to turmoil and lowering your blood pressure.

Classic ADHD is usually very responsive to stimulant medications, such as Ritalin, Dexedrine, Cylert, Desoxyn, and Adderal. These medications "turn on" the frontal lobes and prevent the shutdown which often occurs with ADD.

Additional Symptoms Notes For ADHD:

1. Restless, fidgety
- like a mosquito buzzing around the environment, or a bullet ricocheting off the walls,
- jitterbug, others note excessive movement
- legs or fingers in constant motion
- hyperactivity

2. Problems remaining seated
- up, down, all around
- swinging around in seat
- constantly up

3. Easily distracted by extraneous stimuli
- trouble remaining focused
- hears whatever else is going on
- if someone drops a pencil three rows over, attention immediately goes to the
- pencil and distracts them from their task

4. Problems taking turns

- need to have way immediately
- often tries to cut to the front of the line
- alienates themselves socially from others

5. Responds impulsively or without thinking

- most people have a little brake in their brain that causes them to think before they act; people with ADD seem to be missing that brake and react often without forethought

6. Problems completing things

- homework, school work, chores
- start many things that they do not finish

7. Difficulty with sustained attention or erratic attention

- short attention span for most things
- people with ADD may be able to concentrate on things that are new (sitting in the pediatrician's office), novel, highly interesting (video games) or frightening (dad coming home from work after mom has called him out of a meeting)

8. Shifts from one uncompleted activity to another

- with a short attention span, the ADD person often will go from activity to activity, toy to toy or project to project

9. Difficulty playing quietly

- often described as noisy, loud or intrusive (this may be very difficult for a mother who is sensitive to noise)

10. Talks excessively

- phrases such as "motor mouth," or "who put a quarter in you" are often heard with these people

11. Interrupts frequently

- blurts out answers in class even after being warned not to time after time. Often this is upsetting and embarrassing for parents

12. Doesn't seem to listen

- this may seem somewhat selective, people with ADD often absorb less than 30% of what is said, causing misperception and misinterpretation

13. Disorganization

- book bag
- homework
- room
- desk
- office
- paperwork
- time (often late or in a hurry)
- overall organization is a problem

14. Takes high risks

- these children are at risk for accidents (running into the street without thinking, getting hold of medication that is left out, climbing up cupboards or on top of appliances, etc.)

Additional ADD Symptoms

- often poor handwriting; as adults, they may print
- trouble writing, even though they may be able to say what they are thinking. They have trouble writing what they are thinking (this has been termed finger agnosia)
- often have difficulty getting to sleep and have trouble getting up in the morning
- cannot tune out the edges and concentrate on the middle
- poor memory, scattered
- poor follow through
- homework takes forever
- they tend to be very stimulation-seeking and are experts at getting others angry at them
- easily frustrated
- poor eye tracking
- poor self-esteem, especially with late diagnosis
- chronic failure to master social and academic situations
- unpleasant reaction from others due to their behavior
- suffer from an overdose of criticism
- children are often demoralized and may look depressed
- decreased coordination compared to peers
- many have "soft neurological signs" such as fine motor problems

HALLMARKS OF ADD without Hyperactivity
(helpful indicators for AD/HD, Predominantly Inattentive Type)
(Also Prefrontal Cortex System)

Six or more of the following symptoms are indicative of ADD without hyperactivity.

____ 1. Difficulty with sustained attention or erratic attention span
____ 2. Easily distracted by extraneous stimuli
____ 3. Excessive daydreaming
____ 4. Disorganized
____ 5. Responds impulsively or without thinking
____ 6. Problems completing things
____ 7. Doesn't seem to listen
____ 8. Shifts from one uncompleted activity to another
____ 9. Often complains of being bored
____10. Often appears to be apathetic or unmotivated
____11. Frequently sluggish or slow moving
____12. Frequently spacey or internally preoccupied

The onset of these symptoms often becomes apparent later in childhood or even adolescence. The brighter the individual, the later symptoms seem to become a problem. The symptoms must be present for at least six months and not be related to a depressive episode. The severity of the disorder is rated as mild, moderate or severe. Even though these children have many of the same symptoms of the people with AD/HD, they are not hyperactive and may, in fact, be hypoactive. Girls are frequently missed because they are more likely to have this type of ADD. In addition, they may: daydream excessively, complain of being bored, appear apathetic or unmotivated, appear frequently sluggish or slow moving or appear spacey or internally preoccupied -- the classic "couch potato." Most people with this form of ADD are never diagnosed. They do not exhibit enough symptoms that "grate" on the environment to cause people to seek help for them. Yet, they often experience severe disability from the disorder. Instead of help, they get labeled as willful, uninterested, or defiant. As with the AD/HD subtype, brain studies in patients with ADD, inattentive subtype reveal a decrease in brain activity in the frontal lobes of the brain in response to an intellectual challenge. Again, it seems that the harder these people try to concentrate, the worse it gets. ADD, inattentive subtype is often very responsive to stimulant medications listed above, at a percentage somewhat less than the AD/HD patients.

HALLMARKS OF ADD
Overfocused Type
(Cingulate System)

Six or more of the following symptoms are indicative of ADD overfocused (1 and 2 are needed to make the diagnosis).

___ 1. Difficulty with sustained attention or erratic attention span
___ 2. Easily distracted by extraneous stimuli
___ 3. Excessive or senseless worrying
___ 4. Disorganized or superorganized
___ 5. Oppositional, argumentative
___ 6. Strong tendency to get locked into negative thoughts, having the same thought over and over
___ 7. Tendency toward compulsive behavior
___ 8. Intense dislike for change
___ 9. Tendency to hold grudges
___10. Trouble shifting attention from subject to subject
___11. Difficulties seeing options in situations
___12. Tendency to hold on to own opinion and not listen to others
___13. Tendency to get locked into a course of action, whether or not it is good for the person
___14. Needing to have things done a certain way or becomes very upset
___15. Others complain that you worry too much

People with ADD, overfocused subtype, tend to get locked into things and they have trouble shifting their attention from thought to thought. This subtype has a very specific brain pattern, showing increased blood flow in the top, middle portion of the frontal lobes. This is the part of the brain that allows you to shift your attention from thing to thing. When this part of the brain is working too hard, people have trouble shifting their attention and end up "stuck" on thoughts or behaviors.

This brain pattern may present itself differently among family members. For example, a mother or father with ADD overfocused subtype may experience trouble focusing along with obsessive thoughts (repetitive negative thoughts) or have compulsive behaviors (hand washing, checking, counting, etc.). The son or daughter may be oppositional (get stuck on saying no, no way, never, you can't make me do it), and another family member may find change very hard for them.

This pattern is often very responsive to new "anti-obsessive anti-depressants," which increase the neurotransmitter serotonin in the brain. I have nicknamed these medications as my "anti-stuck medications." These medications include Prozac, Paxil, Zoloft, Anafranil, Luvox and Effexor. When these medications are not helpful, or even seem to make things worse, the new antipsychotic medications can be very helpful. These include Risperdal, Zyprexa and Seroquel.

HALLMARKS OF ADD
Depressive Type
(Deep Limbic System)

Six or more of the following symptoms are indicative of ADD depressive subtype (1 and 2 are needed to make the diagnosis).

___ 1. Difficulty with sustained attention or erratic attention span
___ 2. Easily distracted by extraneous stimuli
___ 3. Moodiness
___ 4. Negativity
___ 5. Low energy
___ 6. Irritability
___ 7. Social isolation
___ 8. Hopelessness, helplessness, excessive guilt
___ 9. Disorganization
___10. Lowered sexual interest
___11. Sleep changes (too much or too little)
___12. Forgetfulness
___13. Low self-esteem

It is very important to differentiate this subtype of ADD from clinical depression. This is best done by evaluating the symptoms over time. ADD, depressive subtype, is consistent over time and there must have been evidence from childhood and adolescence. It does not just show up at the age of 35 when someone is going through serious stress in their life. It must be a pattern of behavior over time. Major depressive disorders tend to cycle. There are periods of normalcy which alternate with periods of depression.

The medications used for ADD, depressive subtype include standard antidepressants, such as Tofranil (imipramine), Norpramin (desipramine), and Pamelor (nortryptiline), the newer antidepressants such as Prozac (fluoxetine), Effexor (venlafaxine) and Wellbutrin (buprion), and the stimulants. Clinically, I have been very impressed with the ability of stimulants to help this subtype of ADD. This is why it is very important to differentiate this subtype from primary depressive disorders.

HALLMARKS OF ADD
Explosive Type
(Temporal Lobes)

Six or more of the following symptoms are indicative of ADD violent, explosive (1 and 2 are needed to make the diagnosis).

___ 1. Difficulty with sustained attention or erratic attention span

___ 2. Easily distracted by extraneous stimuli

___ 3. Impulse control problems

___ 4. Short fuse or periods of extreme irritability

___ 5. Periods of rages with little provocation

___ 6. Often misinterprets comments as negative when they are not

___ 7. Irritability builds, then explodes, then recedes; often tired after a rage

___ 8. Periods of spaciness or confusion

___ 9. Periods of panic or fear for no specific reason

___10. Visual changes, such as seeing shadows or objects changing shape

___11. Frequent periods of deja vu (feelings of being somewhere before even though you never have)

___12. Sensitivity or mild paranoia

___13. History of a head injury or family history of violence or explosiveness

___14. Dark thoughts; may involve suicidal or homicidal thoughts

___15. Periods of forgetfulness or memory problems

In my clinical experience, temporal lobe symptoms are found in approximately 10-15% of patients with ADD. Temporal lobe symptoms can be among the most painful. These include periods of panic or fear for no specific reason, periods of spaciness or confusion, dark thoughts (such as suicidal or homicidal thoughts), significant social withdrawal, frequent periods of deja vu, irritability, rages, and visual changes (such as things getting bigger or smaller than they really are). Temporal lobe dysfunction may be inherited or it may be caused by some sort of brain trauma.

Temporal lobe symptoms associated with ADD are often very responsive to antiseizure medications, such as Tegretol, Neurontin, or Depakote.

HALLMARKS OF ADD
Ring of Fire Type
(Multiple Hot Areas around the Cortex)

Six or more of the following symptoms are indicative of ADD Ring of Fire (1 and 2 are needed to make the diagnosis).

____ 1. Difficulty with sustained attention or erratic attention span
____ 2. Easily distracted by extraneous stimuli
____ 3. Angry or aggressive
____ 4. Sensitive to noise, light, clothes or touch
____ 5. Frequent or cyclic mood changes (highs and lows)
____ 6. Inflexible, rigid in thinking
____ 7. Demanding to have their way, even when told no multiple times
____ 8. Periods of mean, nasty or insensitive behavior
____ 9. Periods of increased talkativeness
____ 10. Periods of increased impulsivity
____ 11. Unpredictable behavior
____ 12. Grandiose or "larger than life" thinking
____ 13. Talks fast
____ 14. Appears that thoughts go fast
____ 15. Appears anxious or fearful

Hallmark symptoms of this type include irritability, hyperactivity, excessive talking, overfocus issues, extreme oppositional behavior, and cyclic periods of calm behavior alternating with intense aggressive behavior. The ring of fire brain pattern shows excessive activity across the whole cortical surface, as opposed to classic ADD which shows decreased activity with concentration. Ring of fire ADD may represent a variant of bipolar disorder and ADD. It is often helped with either anticonvulsant medication or the new antipsychotic medications such as Risperdal or Zyprexa. Stimulant medications often intensify the overactivity and make symptoms worse. St. John's Wort and medications which increase serotonin often make this type much worse.

Conclusion

Depression, anxiety and ADD are, in part, biological disorders and often responsive to effective treatment. In Christine's case above, when she was treated with a combination of psychotherapy, parent training and medication she improved both emotionally and scholastically.

There are many other problems that occur in kids and teenagers, including drug abuse, family problems or eating disorders. The point here is that when a child or teen is showing signs of trouble, rather than ignoring it or blaming them it is important to search for answers.

Of course, even if your child has an underlying emotional or neurological problem this course will be very helpful for you, but it is essential that you seek professional help for your child. Depression, anxiety disorders and ADD are not, I repeat are not, a choice and not their fault!!

Understanding the reasons behind misbehavior will help you be more effective in dealing with it.

Chapter Six

WHY PARENTS STRUGGLE

Children are not the only ones who struggle in the parent-child relationship. Often parents act inappropriately or in an ineffective manner that inadvertently encourages bad behavior. Here are some of the reasons parents struggle.

LACK OF TRAINING

Parenting requires no formal education even though it is one of the most complex and difficult tasks any of us ever do. "Winging it" with kids is not good enough unless you have children who are great at raising themselves.

LACK OF APPROPRIATE ROLE MODELS

Learned behavior is actually stored in the brain. If you never experienced good parenting it is hard to be a good parent without the proper training. Having ineffective parents often teaches bad habits that are unconsciously repeated.

AUTHORITY CONFLICTS

The current generation of parents has serious problems with authority issues. Many of us grew up during the Vietnam War. For many years we frequently saw students and war protesters demonstrating against authority. Authority became a bad word. Because of this I think many modern-day parents have trouble believing that their children should respect them or that being firm is good for children. In addition, many parents get into the trap of wanting to be liked by their children and become unable to exert authority

LOW SELF ESTEEM

Self esteem plays a huge role in parenting. If you have low self-esteem you're likely to believe you'll be a lousy parent and thus act in a way that is consistent with that belief.

STRESS

Parenting skills are very sensitive to stress. Because children are little and weak parents who are stressed can take out their frustrations on them. A bad day at the office for mom or dad often results in the child's being screamed at for little or no reason. Work pressures, financial problems, marital discord or health problems can set up parental difficulties. Everyday stresses as well, interfere with the parent-child relationship. Some of these stresses include: interruptions of plans, minor accidents, pet peeves and trouble with in-laws.

NEGATIVE THINKING PATTERNS

Negative thoughts and assumptions about a child can be very harmful. When a parent assumes the child is misbehaving in order to embarrass him or her, they react in a negative way that almost reinforces bad behavior.

UNDERLYING EMOTIONAL OR NEUROLOGICAL PROBLEMS

49% of adults at some point in their life will experience an emotional or learning problem which will interfere with their ability to effectively parent. (ADD, depression, anxiety, learning disabilities, substance abuse, etc.)

As a parent, having an unrecognized, undiagnosed, untreated mental illness can be devastating to the emotional development of a child. I once had a phone call from a very close friend whom I hadn't heard from in years. He sounded different. When we lived close together he was energetic, positive, outgoing, funny and fascinated by the world around him. As I listened to him on the phone, however, his voice was flat and his thoughts were very negative. He told me his life had no meaning and he would much rather "see heaven" than struggle through any more days. My friend was sleeping a lot, had problems concentrating and even lost interest in sex, which was a real change for him. He was also irritable and aggressive with his child and became socially withdrawn from everyone. He suffered from clinical depression. He was the last person in the world with whom I expected to be having that kind of conversation.

But, mental illness is extremely common. A recent study by the National Institutes of Mental Health demonstrated that 49% of the population will suffer from a mental illness during some point in their life. Anxiety problems, depression and alcohol or drug abuse are the most common problems. Mental illnesses strike the rich and the poor, the successful and the not so successful. They devastate individuals and families, and they most often go untreated because of the stigma our society attaches to them. My friend had postponed calling me for over nine months. It was not until his wife threatened to divorce him that he called me.

If you or someone you know has persistent symptoms it's important to have a psychiatric evaluation by a competent professional. Too often, because of the stigma, it takes child abuse, a broken marriage, a job loss or a life at the brink of suicide before a person seeks help. Our society needs to think of emotional problems as we think of medical problems and teach people to seek help for them much like we would do if we found blood in our urine.

Common emotional illnesses include depression, anxiety disorders and substance abuse. You can imagine how difficult it would be to parent a difficult child if the adult suffered from one of these illnesses.

Attention deficit disorders (ADD) in adults can have devastating effects on the parent-child relationship. The hallmark symptoms of adult ADD are impulsivity, a short attention span, distractibility and restlessness. Until recently, most people thought that children outgrew this disorder during their teenage years. That is false. While it is true that the hyperactive component lessens over time, the other symptoms of impulsivity, distractibility and a short attention span remain for most of these children into adulthood. Current research shows that seventy to eighty percent of these children never fully outgrow this disorder. Imagine how difficult it would be to parent a difficult child if you had these symptoms.

As I mentioned in the last chapter ADD is a neurological problem that affects between three to five percent of the population. When it is left untreated it has serious learning, social and emotional consequences.

In my clinical practice I see many children who have attention deficit disorder. When I meet with their parents and take a good family history I find that there is about a ninety percent chance that at least one of the parents also had symptoms of ADD as a child and may, in fact, still be showing symptoms as an adult. Many of the parents were never diagnosed. One of the most common ways I diagnose ADD in adults is when parents reluctantly tell me that they have tried their child's medication and that they found it very helpful. They report it helped them concentrate for longer periods of time, they became more organized and were less impulsive. Trying a child's medication is not something I recommend.

Other symptoms of the adult form of ADD include: poor organization and planning, procrastination, trouble listening to directions, and excessive traffic violations. Additionally, people with adult ADD are often late for appointments, frequently misplace things, may be quick to anger, and have poor follow through. There may also be frequent, impulsive job changes, and poor financial management. Substance abuse, including alcohol, amphetamines and cocaine, is common. Low self-esteem is often prevalent.

Many people do not recognize the seriousness of this disorder in children or adults and just pass these people off as defiant and willful. Yet, as I mentioned ADD is a serious disorder. If left untreated it affects a person's self-esteem, social relationships and ability to learn.

Many adults tell me that when they were children they were in trouble all the time and had a real sense that there was something very different about them. Even though many of the adults I treat with ADD are very bright they are frequently frustrated by not living up to their potential. Some adults with ADD are successful, but only if they surround themselves with people who organize them.

According to Russell Barkley, Ph.D. of the University of Massachusetts, in order to make the diagnosis of adult ADHD a person must have at least 3 of the following 12 symptoms (5 or 6 symptoms makes this disorder very likely). These symptoms must not be part of another psychiatric disorder, such as substance abuse or depression and they must have been present since childhood.

1. trouble sustaining attention
2. difficulty completing projects
3. easily overwhelmed by tasks of daily living
4. trouble maintaining an organized work/living area
5. inconsistent work performance
6. lacks attention to detail
7. makes decisions impulsively
8. difficulty delaying gratification, stimulation seeking
9. restless, fidgety
10. makes comments without considering their impact
11. impatient, easily frustrated
12. frequent traffic violations

As I mentioned in the last chapter, recent brain imaging studies have shown a clear neurological basis to ADD. When people with ADD try to concentrate their frontal lobes (the part of the brain that controls attention span, impulse control and judgment) decrease in activity, rather than increase in activity which happens in people who do not have ADD. This frontal lobe deactivation helps to explain why kids and adults with ADD stir up their environment and seem to be on the look out for trouble. If they can get someone angry at them the turmoil has a tendency to stimulate their brains and help them feel more normal. The six types of ADD I described in children also apply for adults. Go back through the checklists for yourself or other adults in the child's life to see if they apply.

If you think that you or someone you love has adult ADD it's important to have a thorough evaluation. My bias is that a psychiatrist, especially a child psychiatrist, should do it because they have the most experience with this disorder. Many adult psychiatrists and family physicians have very little experience with ADD and may misdiagnose it. With good treatment ADD is a very treatable disorder in children or adults. Without treatment there are potentially serious consequences in a person's ability to work and to love. When a parent has this disorder it can seriously undermine the parent-child relationship.

In order to effectively parent difficult children parents must look at their own attitudes, behavior and mental health.

Chapter Seven

FINDING THE BEST "FIT"
BETWEEN YOU AND YOUR CHILD

As you can see, there are many factors that are involved with parenting. The goal of effective parenting is often to find the best "fit" between the parent and the child, which involves adapting one's own personality with the child's characteristics given the environment you're in.

Opposed to what many people believe children are not born as "blank slates." They bring their own personalities and characteristics to the parent-child relationship.

A child is born with their own:

- temperament
- sleep-wake cycle
- level of patience or tolerance level
- sensitivity to noise and touch
- resistance to infection
- ability to adapt to change
- need for affection
- ability to bond

Similarly, parents come to the relationship with their child with their own:

- temperament
- sleep-wake cycle
- level of patience or tolerance level
- sensitivity to noise and touch
- resistance to infection
- ability to adapt to change
- need for affection
- ability to bond
- prior experiences with other children
- old parenting "tapes" from their own childhood experiences

In addition, parents have STRESS:

- relationships
- work
- health
- finances
- commuting
- etc.

The following equation will help you think of the complexities of parenting:

Child's Characteristics

+

Parent's Characteristics

+

Social Stresses

=

Fit Between Parent and Child

Here's a dramatic example of how the "interactive fit" can be a problem.

Nine-year-old Philip was frightened when the police came to his school to talk with him about the bruises his teacher noticed on his legs and arms. He wasn't sure if he should tell them that his father had beaten him up, or if he should say he fell down a flight of stairs or something like that. Philip did not want to get his dad in trouble and he felt responsible for the beating he received. After all, he reasoned, his father had told him ten times to clean his room and for some reason, unknown to Philip, he didn't do it. Philip and his father often fought but it had never been apparent to people outside the home. Philip decided to tell the truth, hoping that it would help his family get some help.

Indeed, Philip's family did get help. The court ordered the father to undergo a psychiatric evaluation and counseling for the family. The father was found to have a short fuse and was impulsive and explosive in several different situations. He began to have problems with aggressiveness after he sustained a head injury in a car accident six years ago. His wife reported that when Philip was first born the father was loving, patient and attentive.

In family counseling sessions Philip was noticed to be a very difficult kid. He was restless, active, impulsive and defiant. When his parents would tell him to stop doing annoying behaviors he just ignored them and continued irritating those around him.

The psychiatrist soon discovered it was the interaction between Philip and his father that was the problem and counseling alone would not be helpful. He believed there was some underlying biological or physical cause that contributed to the abusive interactions. Philip and his father were both referred for a brain study in order to further understand the underlying problem.

The brain studies for both Philip and his father were abnormal. The father's study showed an area of increased activity in his left temporal lobe (near his temples), probably a result of the car accident. Several researchers implicate this area of the brain as a problem in people who have a tendency toward violence or a short fuse. Philip's brain study revealed decreased activity in the front part of his brain. This finding is often found in kids who are impulsive and overly active.

When the psychiatrist received the results it was clear to him that Philip's and his father's problems were, in part, biological. He placed both of them on medication. The father was put on anti-seizure medication to calm his left temporal lobe and Philip was placed on medication to increase activity in the front part of his brain.

Once the biological problems were treated the family was able to benefit from family therapy and begin to heal the wounds of abuse. In counseling, Philip was calmer and more attentive and the father was able to learn how to deal with Philip's difficult behavior in a constructive way.

Whenever child abuse occurs it is a tragedy. It may become worse, however, if people ignore underlying problems that may contribute to the difficulties. In this case and in many others, it is the interaction between a difficult child and an aggressive or impulsive parent that leads to the problem. These interactions may have a biological basis. Having a thorough evaluation by a psychiatrist may be necessary if working through this course does not solve the difficult child's problems. For most of you this case may appear extreme. In my experience it isn't.

On a practical, day-to-day basis here are 10 things you can do to improve the interactive fit between you and your child.

1. Optimize your daily cycles. When is your best time of the day? When is your child's best time of the day. Try to spend time together during the overlapping best times.

2. If your child is noisy and you like quiet make sure you have enough of your own "quiet time" so that you can recharge your batteries and be more able to deal with the noise.

3. If both you and the child are stubborn, learn to be flexible. Don't push when you see your child get stuck or locked into a certain position. Two stubborn people is the prescription for turmoil.

4. It is helpful if both the parents and children avoid foods with high sugar contents. Many children are sugar sensitive, an hour or two later exhibiting more irritable, oppositional and cranky behavior (parents happen to be the same way).

5. Make sure you have someone to talk to about the stresses in your life. The better you handle your own stress the less likely you will be to take it out on your children.

6. One of the best suggestions I have given parents over the years to improve the fit between them and their children is to have them exercise together. Exercise has many tangible mental and physical health benefits. When parents do it with their children everyone notes a calming air around the house.

7. Read your goals everyday (both parents and kids) to stay focused on how important this relationship is to each of you individually.

8. Lots of hugs, even if the child is sensitive to touch. The more touching, hugging, connecting, often the more relaxed people in a family feel.

9. When a parent comes home from work give them 20-30 minutes of alone time, if needed, to collect themselves before having to check homework, get dinner ready, or do chores. Time to rest and clear your head is essential to being successful.

10. Everyone needs to learn how to breathe slowly when things are getting out of control. I'll talk more about this later in the course. For now, whenever you get upset take a big breath in, hold it for 2 seconds, then very slowly exhale for between 5-10 seconds. Getting control of your breathing is the first step to controlling your actions to fit your goals. Without enough oxygen to our brain our behavior suffers (subsequently our kids suffer).

Chapter Eight

THINKING CLEARLY AND LOGICALLY
WHEN DEALING WITH YOUR CHILD

Parenting requires clear thinking. It is especially important in raising difficult kids. When you have dealt with a difficult child year after year your thoughts and expectations become negative and you decrease your chances to step back to take a realistic look at the situation. Correcting negative thoughts will be very helpful.

Did you know that every time you have a thought, every single time you have a thought your brain releases chemicals. That is how our brain works. We have a thought, our brain releases chemicals, an electrical transmission goes across our brain and we become aware of what we are thinking. These brain chemicals influence every part of your body. Whenever you have an angry thought, a hopeless thought, a depressing thought or a frightening thought, your brain releases a certain set of chemicals that cause your whole body to react and feel bad. Think about the last time you were really angry at your child. What happened in your body almost immediately? If you're like most people you probably noticed that your muscles became tighter, your breathing rate increased, your hands began to sweat and become colder and your heart rate increased. This is the operating principal behind polygraphs or lie detector tests -- your body reacts to what you think.

On the other hand, every time you have a positive thought, a happy thought, a hopeful thought, a successful thought, a pleasant thought (I often think of my five year old who is very active, a thought of her asleep), your brain releases a completely different set of chemicals that make you feel good, and make you feel relaxed and give your body actually the opposite response where your heart goes slower, your hands get warmer, they get drier and your muscles get relaxed. So what you think is critical to how you feel and what you do.

In parenting, it's necessary not to just accept what you think. Recognize the thoughts that go through your head and correct them when they are distorted or replace them with positive thoughts when they are negative. You are what you think!

When you don't question the negative thoughts that travel through your brain, your unconscious mind automatically believes them and they could ruin your whole day.

Here are six different ways we distort situations with our children to make them out to be worse than they really are. I call these ANTs (automatic negative thoughts). They can invade you like ants invading a kitchen. When you recognize and talk back to these ANTs you'll be able to deal with difficult situations much more effectively.

The first type of "thought distortion" is something called **overgeneralization**: That is where you take one event and view it as something that will always repeat itself. For example, if your child talks back to you you might think to yourself, "He's always got a smart mouth!" Or if the child doesn't do her chores you think, "She never does what I tell her to do!" Whenever you find yourself thinking in words such as always, everyone, never, every time, those are overgeneralizations and usually incorrect or distorted thoughts. The problem with negative thoughts is that if you never challenge them you believe them a 100%. Then you act from your thought beliefs rather than the truth of the situation. If you really believe that your child "always" has a smart mouth you're likely to go into a rage at them, when in reality it may only be 5-10% of the time.

Fortune telling is another type of thought distortion. This is where you arbitrarily predict things will turn out badly, even though you have no definite evidence. An example of this in parenting occurs when you predict that your child won't mind you in a situation and you become angry with them even before you leave home. No one can predict the future. Unless you're a contract lawyer there is no good reason to focus on predicting the worst. Predicting the worst can actually set it up to happen through unconscious mental mechanisms. For example, if you predict that the child will not do the dishes properly. You might start to nag him to the point where he gets angry and doesn't do them to spite you. I'm not telling you to always have a "pie-in-the-sky" attitude toward your children. It is important to check and follow through with them. But predicting the worst will generally make the situation worse.

Mind reading is similar to fortune telling. This is where you arbitrarily predict what the child is thinking before you have checked it out. As I mentioned in the development chapter, children often do not know why they do what they do. Yet, when they misbehave parents often attribute negative motives to the child. I've heard parents tell me, "My son is trying to embarrass me. He knows what he's doing and he likes it when I'm upset." You cannot read another person's mind, children have enough trouble reading their own minds.

Having a **negative filter** is yet another way we distort situations: In this, everything is filtered through negativeness: only the bad in situations is focused on. I once had a patient who recently moved to the area before she saw me. She had 80% of her house put away from the move. She didn't focus on that, however. The only part she could think about was the 20% that wasn't put away. She told me that she was 100% inadequate, 100% inferior, and 100% disorganized. Even though she was caring for three small children, she could only see what she hadn't done rather than what she had done. When you have a negative filter you often discount any successes or positive experiences. Often, when parents of difficult kids have a good day they discount the experience and predict things will quickly turn sour again.

Labeling is very harmful to children. Often parents give very negative labels to difficult children not knowing that they are unconsciously programming the child to become more negative. For example, when you call your child a spoiled brat or an idiot you lump them with all the "spoiled brats" and "idiots" that you've ever known and you inhibit your ability to take a realistic view of the child. Stay away from negative labels. In addition, if the child is a "spoiled brat" it is probably not her fault. It was the parents who did the spoiling.

Guilt thinking is prevalent among many parents and it is uniformly destructive. Guilt thinking occurs when parents beat themselves up with words like "should, must, ought to and have to." These words are not helpful in making you feel more positive or connected to your child. It is much better to replace the "shoulds" with phrases such as "It would be helpful for me...It is in my child's best interest to do this...It fits my goals of having a better relationship to do this....etc."

The first step to changing your perceptions or thinking patterns is to identify the way you do think. Whenever you notice a self-critical or distorted thought entering your mind, train yourself to recognize it and write it down. When you write down negative thoughts and talk back to them, you begin to take away their power and gain control over your moods.

For example:

Negative Thought	Distortion	Talk Back
My child never does anything right.	Overgeneralization	That's not true. She does Many things right, it's just hard for me to notice them at times.

Buy yourself a notebook and carry it with you wherever you go. Whenever you note one of these distorted thoughts coming in, write it down, identify it, then talk back to it. The power in this method is tremendous. It not only will help you correct distorted perception, it will also help your mood, self-esteem, and your ability to deal with your child in a rational and more effective way.

Chapter Nine

CLEAR STEPS TO DRAMATICALLY IMPROVE THE QUALITY OF YOUR RELATIONSHIP WITH YOUR CHILD

The quality of the relationship with your child sets the tone for the whole parenting experience. It is often the single most important factor in a child's development. If you have a good relationship with a child almost any form of discipline will work. If you have a bad relationship with a child almost nothing works.

When you have a difficult child your relationship with them often suffers. Many mothers have told me that they feel like running away from home to avoid the constant turmoil at home. Parents of a difficult child are often filled with guilt and frustration because what they are doing with the child isn't working! Repairing the relationship with a child has to occur before you can effectively parent them.

In order to repair or enhance the relationship between you and your child take an inventory of how you interact with them.

There are many qualities that enhance a positive relationship between a parent and a child. List five:

1. _____

2. _____

3. _____

4. _____

5. _____

Think about the worst bosses you have ever had and list five of their characteristics:

1. _____

2. _____

3. _____

4. _____

5. _____

Now, think about the best bosses you have ever had and list five of their characteristics:

1. _____

2. _____

3. _____

4. _____

5. _____

As a parent you are the child's supervisor. Does your behavior fit in the "good boss" category or the "bad boss" category?

Here is a list of "good versus bad supervisors" that I have collected from my parenting classes over the years.

Good Supervisor	Bad Supervisor
--supportive	--can't trust
--gives time to teach	--expects you to know things not taught
--leads by example	--example is opposite of what is expected
--positive attitude	--poor attitude towards work
--expects you'll do well	--expects you'll screw up
--pleasant to be around	--a real drag to be around
--feel like you can talk to him or her without being ridiculed	--afraid to talk to him or her for fear of ridicule or embarrassment
--notices employees for particularly good work	--only mistakes are noticed
--honest	--dishonest
--predictable	--unpredictable
--communicates clear, reasonable expectations	--gives vague expectations, over tasks
--gives honest feedback	--no feedback till trouble
--admits mistakes	--blames others
--takes time to find out	--jumps to conclusions
--fair	--shows favoritism
--patient	--impatient, too critical
--allows privacy and space	--intrusive/nosy

I once did this "best boss versus worst boss" exercise with a man who was being harassed by his boss. When he told me about his difficult 14 year old I asked him if he treated him as a good supervisor or a bad one. The father started to cry. He saw very similar traits between himself as a father and the boss who was making him angry at work. As he understood his negative behavior toward his son he was able to change it and redirect his energy in a more positive way.

This list translates well into the characteristics of good versus bad parenting characteristics.

Good Parent	Bad Parent
--supportive	--doesn't seem to care
--loving	--acts like they dislike their children
--there for their children	--unavailable to them
--able to receive gifts from children	--ridicules or downplays gifts given to them by their children
--gives time to teach	--too busy for them
--whenever possible, allows children to make their own decisions	--has to make decisions for them
--praises independent actions of children	--ridicules independent actions by children
--leads by example	--their words and actions don't match up
--firm	--too lenient
--clear expectations	--confusing expectations
--consistent	--unpredictable
--good sense of humor	--too serious
--enjoyable to be around	--a drain to be around
--admits mistakes	--blames others, especially children
--takes time to find out information	--jumps to conclusions
--fair	--shows favoritism
--patient	--impatient, too critical
--allows privacy and space	--intrusive/nosy
--encourages children to do their best	--competes with their children
--conveys to children an expectation they'll succeed	--children know they expect them to fail
--children feel they can talk to them without being ridiculed	--children afraid to talk to them for fear of ridicule or embarrassment
--notices good behavior	--only bad behavior is noticed
--gives honest feedback in a way that can be heard	--no feedback till trouble
--not always serious, can use humor to lighten the atmosphere	--always serious, never acts like a real person

Go over these two lists and circle the ways you treat your kids. List the number from the good side versus the number from the bad side and circle it.

good   versus   # bad

Two Critical Ingredients for Great Relationships

The essential ingredients for building positive relationships with children include: time together and a willingness to listen.

Time

A study published in USA Today in the late 1980s reported that "on average, parents spend less than 7 minutes a week talking with their children. It is not possible to have much of a relationship on such little time. Children need actual, physical time with their parents. Think about times your parents spent positive one-on-one time with you. Did that make you feel important, special?

Some parents complain that their children are too busy or are not interested in spending time with them. When this happens I recommend parents force the issue with their kids, telling them that they're important to them and that they need to spend time with them. Of course, the way in which you spend time with them is critical. If you spend the time lecturing or interrogating them, neither of you will find it very enjoyable and both of you will look for ways to avoid contact in the future.

Here is an exercise that I've found extremely powerful in improving the quality time you have with your child. The exercise is called "SPECIAL TIME." SPECIAL TIME works. Do it as I suggest and it will improve the quality of the relationship with your child in a very short period of time. Here are the directions for SPECIAL TIME.

** Spend 20 minutes a day with the child doing something that he or she would like to do. It's important to approach the child in a positive way and say something like, "I feel we have not had enough time together and you're important to me. Let's spend some special time together every day. What would you like to do?" It's important to remember that the purpose of this time is to build the relationship with your child. Keep it as positive as possible.

** During the special time together there is to be no parental commands, no questions and no directions. This is very important. This is a time to build the relationship, not discipline difficult behavior. If, for example, you're playing a game and the child starts to cheat -- you cheat and reframe their behavior. You can say something like, "I see you've changed the rules of the game and I'll play by your rules." Remember the goal of special time is to improve the relationship between you and your child, not to teach. Of course, at other times if the child cheats it is important to deal with it.

** Notice as many positive behaviors as you can. Noticing the good is much more effective in shaping behavior than noticing the bad.

** Do much more listening than talking.

I once received a phone call from a friend of mine who complained that his 18 month old daughter did not want anything to do with him when he came home from work. He told me that he thought it must be "one of those mother-daughter things" and that she'd probably grow out of it. I told him that it probably meant he wasn't spending enough time with his daughter and that if he did SPECIAL TIME with his daughter that she would become much more open and affectionate with him. My friend took my advice. He spent 20 minutes a day doing something that his daughter chose (usually playing blocks in her room). He spent the time listening to her and feeding back what he heard her say. Within 3 weeks, his daughter's behavior dramatically changed. Whenever my friend would come home from work his daughter would run to hug him and she hung on his leg all evening.

Remember, actual, physical, daily time between a parent and a child will have a powerfully positive effect on the relationship.

SPECIAL TIME

Is The Best Investment You Can Make With Your Children

(It will pay off for the rest of their lives)

A Willingness to Listen

Good communication is essential to any relationship and absolutely essential to the difficult parent-child relationship. In order to get your child to talk with you, you must first show that you are willing to accept and listen to what they have to say. You must also believe that they have the capacity to solve many of their own problems if they are allowed to talk through them. "Active Listening" with children and teens works to increase the level of communication. The concept of "Active Listening" is simple: repeat back what you hear before you react and listen for the feelings behind the words (this is also great for adult relationships).

Too often parents are telling children how to think before they really understand the situation. This behavior cuts off communication and decreases the chances that the child will come to you in the future.

Here's an example of active listening and bad listening.

1. Initially, accept what is said without judging the content of the words.

Teen: I would like to paint my hair blue.
(inflammatory statement)

Ineffective Parent: Not as long as you live in my house!
(ends the conversation or starts a fight)

Effective Parent: You want to paint your hair blue?
(and then he or she stays quiet long enough for the child to explain).

2. Listen for the feelings behind the words.

Teen: All the kids are wearing their hair that way.
(as if he has somehow taken a scientific poll)

Ineffective Parent: I don't care what anyone else does, you're not going to have blue hair. If they are going to jump off a bridge are you going to go with them.
(again, this sets up a fight with the teen or causes them to withdraw.)

Effective Parent: Sounds like you want to be like the other kids. (encourages understanding and further communication)

3. Reflect back what you hear the child saying and feeling.

The teen might then respond: Sometimes I feel like I don't fit in, maybe changing my appearance will help.

Ineffective Parent: Don't be silly. Of course, you fit in. Your appearance has nothing to do with it!

Effective Parent: You think your appearance prevents you from fitting in.

By responding in a positive reflective way you encourage communication. When you respond in a harsh, condescending or critical way you decrease communication which may cause a sense of loneliness and alienation in a child or teen.

In my parenting classes, many parents report that they never felt listened to when they were a child. They often talk about feeling discounted, misunderstood, frustrated, angry and cut off. Not being listened to harmed their relationship. On the other side, there are parents who talk about special times when they really felt their parents were really listening to what they had to say. Here the feelings were very strong: they felt as though their opinion mattered, they felt understood, and they were much more willing to talk with their parents in the future.

One parent told a class about a time when she threw a glass at her brother and cut his face. She was surprised when her mother sincerely wanted to hear what had gone on instead of just yelling at her. "Even though I received a spanking for what I did," she said, "I felt my mother really listened to me about how my brother was teasing me before I lost control and not just placing the blame on me. It made me want to go to her in the future because I knew she'd listen." Feeling as though someone is listening to what you have to say is critical to a good relationship and encourages communication.

Here are other **communication pitfalls** to avoid with your kids:

1. Poor attitude. This is where you expect the conversation to go no where and subsequently you don't even try to direct it in a positive way.

2. Negative Assumptions about the child. Up front you don't trust what the child or teen will tell you and you remain stiff and guarded during the time together.

3. No reinforcing body language. Body language is so important because it sends conscious and unconscious messages. When a parent and a child are having a discussion and one person fails to make eye contact or acknowledge the other person with facial or body gestures the person who is talking begins to feel lost, alone and unenthusiastic about continuing the conversation. Eye contact and physical acknowledgment is essential to good communication.

4. Competing with distractions. Distractions frequently doom communication. It's not a good idea, for example, to try to communicate when the child is watching their favorite TV show or when they are in the middle of a video game.

5. Never asking for feedback on what you're saying. Many people assume that they are sending clear messages to their child and become upset when the child doesn't do what was asked. Many difficult kids have poor attention spans or poor listening skills, it's often important to ask them to repeat back what you said in order to clarify they really understood your command.

6. Kitchen sinking. This occurs in arguments when a parent feels backed into a corner and he or she brings up unrelated issues from the past in order to protect themselves or intensify the disagreement. Stay on task until an issue is fully discussed.

7. Mind reading. This is where you arbitrarily predict what the child or teen is thinking and then react on that "imagined" information. Checking is very important

8. Sparring. Using put downs, sarcasm, or discounting the child or teens ideas erodes meaningful dialogue and sets up distance in the relationships.

9. Lack of persistence. Often with a child it takes repeated efforts at communication. It's very important not to give up. Remember, kids do not think like adults and parents may need to keep trying at communication.

Time and a willingness to listen are essential ingredients for building great relationships with your children.

Chapter Ten

ESTABLISHING CLEAR FAMILY RULES AND VALUES

Establishing clear, written rules and expectations is the next step in good parenting. These rules need to give direction for the child's behavior. When they know what is expected of them they are much more likely to be able to give it to you. Too often parents believe that children should know how to act without the rules being clearly communicated to them.

Another reason to have the rules written is that children respond to symbols of rules in the environment (traffic signals, posted rules at the pool, etc.) As opposed to how often adults follow the 65 mile per hour speed limit, children are often rule oriented and respond to signs. My nephew Andrew went through a time when he was 3 years old where he was afraid of monsters in his room at night. Week after week Andrew's parents searched the room with Andrew, trying to prove to him that there were no monsters in his room. They looked under the bed, in the closet, behind the door and under the covers. Finally, they realized that they were only making the fear worse by exploring the room for the monsters. Andrew's mother decided that they would make a sign saying that monsters were not allowed in Andrew's room. She and Andrew drew a picture of a monster and then drew a red circle around it with a slash across the monster. Underneath the picture they wrote "NO MONSTERS ALLOWED." Amazingly, Andrew's fear of monsters in his room vanished because he knew the sign kept them away.

Written rules have power! They let children know what is expected of them in a clear way. They allow you to know when the children are following the rules and they give you a basis for reinforcing them, and they also clearly allow you to know when they are not following the rules and serve as a touchpoint for clear, unemotional consequences.

Here is a set of rules that I've found helpful (both for my own household and for my patients). Post them up where the family can see them every day.

FAMILY RULES

1. TELL THE TRUTH

2. TREAT EACH OTHER WITH RESPECT
(this means no yelling, hitting, kicking, name calling, or put downs)

3. NO ARGUING WITH PARENTS
(as parents we want and value your input and ideas, but arguing means you have made your point more than one time)

4. RESPECT EACH OTHER'S PROPERTY
(which means we ask permission to use something that does not belong to us)

5. DO WHAT MOM AND DAD SAY THE FIRST TIME, without complaining or throwing a fit

6. ASK PERMISSION BEFORE YOU GO SOMEWHERE

7. PUT THINGS AWAY THAT YOU TAKE OUT

8. WE LOOK FOR WAYS TO BE KIND AND HELPFUL TO EACH OTHER

Let's take a look at each rule or value statement.

Rule No. 1: Tell the truth. Honesty is a very important value in our family. If you break that rule, you not only get in trouble for doing what you shouldn't have done, but you also get in trouble for lying. The rule is very clear: Tell the truth! This includes little lies and big ones. I've found that when you allow a child to get away with the little lies, the bigger ones are easier to do. One of the best gifts you can give a child is to teach them to be honest in their lives. If they can be honest with the world, they are more likely to be honest with themselves. Of course, this means if you want children to follow this rule you cannot tell lies. Children do what you do, not what you tell them to do. When someone calls, DO NOT tell your child to tell the person you aren't home when you do not want to talk to them. That's a lie and teaches kids that lying is OK.

Rule No. 2: We treat each other with respect. Respect for our fellow person is a very important value. Respect is needed to develop good relationships with others. Relating to others in a positive way is a skill many children (and adults) lack. Disrespect breeds conflict, social isolation, and loneliness. When you don't treat others with respect, there are consequences. When you relate to others in a positive, respectful manner you will attract many more positive things in your life. Teaching this lesson to children early will save them years of frustration.

Rule No. 3: Do what Mom and Dad say the first time. I love this rule! This is my favorite rule! Authority is good! It is necessary. It is helpful. It makes kids feel secure. Yet, for those of us who grew up in the 60s, who saw people demonstrating against the Vietnam War every night on television, we have some ambivalence about authority! We're not quite sure that it's a good thing, so as a generation we've become permissive. What is worse, we've become ambivalent - sometimes we're tough and sometimes we're not! This can cause real problems for children!

Ten thousand children were evaluated in a study looking at parenting styles. Those parents who were permissive had the most problems with their children! The parents who were firm, in a kind way, had the least problems with children. To be an effective parent it is necessary to expect your child to do something the very first time you tell her. Parents often come into my office and say they have to tell their child to do something eight to twelve times! In my mind I'm thinking, "Who's the dummy in this situation?!" If you tell the child to do something eight times and then you get upset, what are you teaching the child? You're teaching the child that it's okay to disobey until the parent goes nuts!

Let me give you an example from my home. When I would tell my son, Anton, to take out the trash, if he doesn't start moving within a reasonable period of time, say 10 seconds, I'd give him a warning. "Yo! Did you hear me? You can do it now, or you can take this consequence, and then you'll get to do it. I don't care; it's up to you." I trained him I was serious the very first time. When you have the expectation that they're going to obey you and you are willing to back it up, they'll get the message and start to obey (unless there are other problems, which we'll discuss later).

Authority is very important, which leads me to:

Rule No. 4: No arguing with parents. I created this rule because many children continually argue with their parents. One child in my practice had the nickname of "Argueman" because he would say the opposite of whatever his parents said to him. In parentheses is, "We really want to hear what you have to say, but we only want to hear it ONCE." Some children are born to argue. They will just go after you and after you and after you and after you. If you let them continually argue with you, guess who else they go after -- their teachers and other people in authority. Arguing is not desirable! If you want to raise healthy kids, authority is a very important element.

Rule No. 5: Respect each other's property. This means you don't take things out of your sister's room. It prevents a lot of fights. This rule encompasses prolonged borrowing, sticky fingers, and stealing. Again, it is important to have this rule written and to enforce consequences when the rule is broken. Many parents ask me what to do if a child is caught stealing from a store. I tell them to take the child back to the store. Have the child confess what he or she did to the store manager. Return the item to the store and pay the store manger the value of the item taken, as a way to compensate the store for the trouble. This technique really gets a child's attention and decreases the chances that stealing will be a problem in the future. When a child steals or breaks something of someone else's at home I recommend that the child be held accountable for that item and pay (in money or work) for the item to be replaced. Making children accountable for their behavior will help solidify clear values.

Rule No. 6: Put things away that you take out. I believe in accountability. Often, mothers in our generation are doing way too much for their children. They have trouble delegating. They do everything, and then they end up angry, burned out, frustrated, and depressed. I think it's extraordinarily important to teach children how to work, and that starts at home, when we get them to help.

There is a large ongoing 50-year-old study at Harvard University which is looking at 450 inner-city Boston school kids, who are now in their 60s. The study is looking for the social causes of depression, alcoholism, anxiety disorders and a variety of other mental health related illnesses. The study is also looking at self-esteem. The only factor, out of 400 variables examined, which correlated with self-esteem was whether or not the children worked as teenagers - worked at home, caring for other children or caring for the house, or worked outside of the house. It is BAD to do everything for a child, because if you do everything for a child, they do not develop self-esteem. Having them put away the things which they take out and having them help around the house is very important to their own mental health. It's also very important to start this principle early. If you do everything for them and then ask them to help at the age of 12, they're going to have heartburn, because they're not used to helping! You're more likely to get the behavior you want when you communicate your expectations to the child.

Rule No. 7: Ask permission before you go somewhere. Proper supervision is essential to a child's emotional well-being. Even though many children complain about it, parents need to check on where children are at, who they are with, and what they are doing. Periodically, physically check that a child (or teen) is where they said that they'll be.

Rule No. 8: Look for ways to be kind and helpful to each other. As you can imagine, with many siblings, that is not a natural state of being. In fact, for those of you who have more than one child, and especially for those of you who have three children, sibling rivalry is alive and well. I'm not exactly sure why siblings have so much trouble, but if you look at the first story of siblings in the Bible, it didn't turn out so well! Sibling rivalry is a natural state of being. When you make it a value, a rule, a part of the family culture to be kind and helpful it will happen more often. When you praise or reward a child for going out of his or her way to be kind and helpful to others you solidify this trait in them.

These rules set the tone and "values" for the family. They clearly state that there is a line of authority at home, and that it is expected that children will follow the rules and respect their parents, their siblings and the family's property. These are good social expectations and teachings. When you tell someone what you expect you're much more likely to get it.

Chapter Eleven

GIVING EFFECTIVE COMMANDS

In parenting children, especially difficult ones it is essential to give them clear commands and direction. This will improve the odds that they will do what you ask them. Communication experts discuss two types of commands: alpha (good) and beta (ineffective).

Beta Commands (ineffective)

1. Chain commands -- too many commands strung together (children with short attention spans may only be able to handle one or two commands at a time.

2. Interrupted commands -- give a command and then have a long discussion before the child is to carry it out.

3. Repeated commands -- this equals nagging.

4. Vague commands -- unclear directions often lead to nothing being done.

5. Question commands -- "Would you please do this?" when it's really not a question.

6. Let's do it together commands -- offering to do a chore or command with a child when they have refused. This positively reinforces him or her for not complying with your command.

7. Psychotwister commands -- these commands have an extremely inappropriate message attached to them. For instance, "If you don't do that I'm going to leave you, send you away, kill myself, etc."

Alpha Commands (effective)

1. Make sure that when you give a chore or a direction that you mean what you say and that the child gets the clear message that you are willing to back it up with consequences if it doesn't get done.

2. Do not present commands as a question or as a favor unless you mean it that way. State the command simply but directly.

3. Do not give too many commands at once.

4. Make sure the child is paying attention to you when the command is given. It's often a good idea to establish eye contact with them.

5. Be sure all distracters in the room are reduced or removed completely. Difficult kids are often very distractible and lessening the distractions increases you chances for compliance.

6. If you're unsure whether your child has understood the command, have him repeat it back to you.

7. If the command is complex or the child traditionally has trouble doing it the way you like, write down on a 3X5 card all the steps involved in doing the task. For example,

   A CLEAN ROOM MEANS: BED MADE, DRAWERS CLOSED, CLOTHES AND TOYS OFF THE FLOOR, AND NOTHING UNDERNEATH THE BED (this makes it easy to check and reward when done right)

If these seven steps are followed, remarkable improvement in a difficult child's compliance can occur.

Chapter Twelve

AVOIDING COMMON PARENTING TRAPS

Without clear thought and guidance, most people raise their children the way their parents raised them. It's this automatic or reflexive nature of parenting that causes many people to fall into "parenting traps." These traps hinder the parent-child relationship. Understanding and avoiding these pitfalls will help you to be more effective with your children.

1. Negative Trap A: A parent gives a child a command; the child yells, whines, complains or throws a tantrum and the parent gives up.

parent gives command-----child noncompliance-----parent gives up

By giving in to a child's noncompliance and misbehavior you've just taught the child it's OK not to do what you've said. When you tell a child to do something, it's important to mean what you say, and make sure the child complies with your direction.

2. Negative Trap B: A parent gives a child a command; the child yells, whines, complains, or throws a tantrum; the parent raises his or her voice and repeats the command; then the child increases the yelling or tantrum; the parent then yells or threatens and finally the child complies.

parent gives command----child noncompliance----parent raises voice, repeats command----child increases noncompliance----parent yells, threatens----child complies

Even though in this trap parents are not giving in to the child's noncompliance, it takes the parent getting angry and repeating commands many times before the child complies. I believe it's very important for children to be taught to comply after being told one time, without a hassle. If you have this as your expectation you'll be able to train this in your children.

3. Positive Trap: A parent gives a child a command; the child yells, whines, complains or throws a tantrum and the parent gives the child a lot of attention explaining why he or she needs to do that certain thing.

parent gives command-----child noncompliance-----parent talks with child (tries to reason, explain, understand).

This is a trap because the child is getting positive attention for misbehavior. Give kids attention for when they comply with your commands, not when they fight you.

4. Split Trap: This occurs when parents allow children to split parental authority. Like adults, children want to have power. If they're allowed to split their parents and have their parents fight over them, then they gain tremendous power and are able to do more and more things. However, this power is not without cost; when children cause their parents to fight they often feel significant guilt. The best parenting occurs when parents agree on how to raise their children and communicate effectively with each other.

5. Delay Trap: Delaying punishment or the "wait until your father gets home" syndrome is ineffective. When you think about consequences for misbehavior it's usually most helpful to punish as soon after the offense as possible. When mothers or fathers threaten the child with the other parent it not only undermines their own authority; it also erodes the child's relationship with the other parent.

6. Broken Promises Trap: Making promises you may not be able to keep. It's very important for parents to keep promises to children. Children learn a sense of trust from their families. If families are predictable and honest, children grow up with a feeling of security and trust. I realize that for extenuating reasons not all promises can be kept. Whenever a promise is broken, however, it's important for parents to find a way to make it up to the child.

7. Faulty Reward Trap: Reward systems are often very helpful in shaping a child's behavior. Yet many parents use rewards that the child is not interested in working for or that take too long to get, such as, "If you clean your room for a month you'll be able to spend a weekend with Uncle Fred." First of all, if the child has never before cleaned his or her room it might be better to start out with a small reward after a few days. It would also be important to know if the child liked

Uncle Fred before you decided to use him as a reward. In setting up reward systems it's essential to have the child's input.

8. Negative Attention Trap: Giving attention for negative behavior, with little or no attention for positive behavior. Children crave attention from their parents. If they can't get it in a positive way, they know they can get it in a negative way. What is the bulk of interactions with your child? If it is usually negative, ask yourself how much praise and positive attention you give your child.

Avoiding these traps will decrease the "stress and yelling" level at home between you and your children and help you to feel good about your ability to raise responsible children.

Chapter Thirteen

REINFORCING YOUR CHILD'S POSITIVE BEHAVIOR

Once you have developed clear goals and expectations for your child it is critical to reinforce their good behavior if you want it to continue. When I think of acceptable behavior the image of boundaries comes to mind, like in a playing field. When the child's behavior is appropriate he or she is within the boundaries, when their behavior becomes inappropriate they are outside of the boundaries. If you reinforce them when their behavior is within the appropriate boundaries their behavior is more likely to stay there. Giving them clear, unemotional consequences when their behavior is outside appropriate boundaries is necessary to nudge them back in.

Learning how to reinforce good behavior is many times more important then learning how to discipline bad behavior. Disciplining difficult behavior only stops bad behavior temporarily. It does not teach them anything new. When you reinforce new, positive behaviors they become stronger, more developed.

I'm a little embarrassed to tell you that I collect penguins. I now have over 800 penguins in my office. Sometimes people come into my office and wonder how I can help them with their stability when I'm a grown man who collects penguins. This is the story behind the penguins.

I did my child psychiatry training in Hawaii, on the Island of Oahu. Outside of Honolulu is Sea Life Park, a marine wild life park like Sea World. One day, in an attempt to be a good dad, I spent the day there with my son, who was 7 at the time. In about the middle of the day we went to the penguin show. The penguin's name was Fat Freddy. Freddy was fabulous. He was a real performer and did amazing things. He jumped off of a 20-foot board into the water below. He bowled with his nose. He counted. He even jumped through a hoop of fire. I was really taken with this penguin.

Toward the end of the show the trainer asked Freddy to get something. Right away Freddy went to get it and brought it back to the trainer. I was a little taken back when I saw this. I thought to myself, "I ask this kid to get me something for me and he wants to have a discussion about it for 20 minutes, and then he doesn't want to do it. What's the difference? I know my son is smarter than this penguin." After the show, I went up to the trainer to ask her how she got Freddy to do all of those really neat things. The trainer looked at my son and then she looked at me and she said, "Unlike parents, whenever Freddy does anything like what I want him to do I notice him, I give him a hug, and then I give him a fish."

Even though my son didn't like fish a light turned on in my head: whenever he did things that I liked I paid no attention to him at all because I'm a very busy guy. But whenever he did something I didn't like I gave him a lot of attention because I didn't want to raise bad kids. Guess what I was doing? I was encouraging him to be a pain in the neck as a way to get my attention.

I collect penguins as a way to remind myself to notice the good things about the people in my life a lot more than the bad things about the people in my life. What do you think Fat Freddy would have done if he was having a bad day and didn't go get the object the trainer asked him to get, and the trainer said, "You stupid penguin. I never met a penguin as dumb as you. We ought to ship you out to the Antarctic and get a replacement." If Freddy would have understood her he would have bit her, or he would have gone off to a corner and cried, depending on his temperament. That would not have been a very helpful response on the part of the trainer. She wouldn't be very effective in training Freddy. But what do you do when someone you love doesn't do what you want them to do right away? Do you trash them emotionally? Do you criticize them? Threaten them? It is much more helpful to notice what you like a lot more than what you don't like.

Several years ago I had a teenager in my office. I had been treating her for depression and ADD. Over two years, she had gotten a lot better, but still had a very difficult relationship with her mother. I also thought her mother had ADD. Her mother was very conflict seeking. On this one day she was crying her eyes out. She and her mother had had a terrible month, fighting nearly everyday. In the middle of crying she looked around my office and said, "Dr. Amen, tell me why does a grown man collect penguins?" I said, "After two years you're just noticing the penguins?" Then I went on to tell her the story of Fat Freddy. In the middle of the story I got an idea. After I was finished I suggested that we "shape" the behavior of her mother. "Let's keep this a secret," I said. "For the next month, every time your mother is appropriate with you, listens to you, is helpful for you, I want you to give her a hug, tell her you love her and say that she's the best mom you could have. Every time she screams at you, yells at you inappropriately or tries to start a fight with you I want you to keep your mouth shut and not say anything." She got a small smile on her face like she understood what I was trying to teach her. She said, "I'm not sure I can do that." I replied, "I know it'll be hard, but for one month let's see what'll happen. What you're doing now isn't going so well." She said she would try. The next month when she came back for her appointment she said she had the best month she had ever had with her mother. She had given her lots of hugs and only had to keep her mouth shut on one occasion when her mom was "going off," as she put it. I taught her how to have personal power by shaping the behavior of her mother. Emotionally, she was now in a much more powerful position than being the victim of her mother's anger.

It is very helpful, whether it is a penguin or something else, to get something in front of your face everyday to remind you how you want to act and behave. Otherwise your unconscious tapes from your parents or your teachers or your coaches or your past or whatever automatically flip on and you just play it. It can be frightening to hear yourself say the same words that your mother or father said to you. My daughter was crying several years ago and I actually heard myself saying to her, "Would you like something to cry about?" Then I went and told her I was sorry and held her.

Rewards or reinforcers may take many forms. As adults we often work for monetary gain. The more financial benefit, the harder we'll work. But we also work for praise from our boss or spouse. Our personality often determines the rewards we're interested in working toward. Children are the same way -- some children will work hard to comply for the verbal praise of their parents, others need different types of rewards. Here is a list of different reinforcers.

Social rewards: verbal praise, "I really like it when you...."
       physical affection, such as hugs or looks

Material rewards: toys
       food, "clean your room before your snack"
       little presents or surprises

Activity rewards: sports
       trips to library, park, arcade

Token rewards: star or point systems
       money
Here are some simple principles in rewarding good behavior:

- use many more rewards than punishments

- reward as soon as possible after the child fulfills your expectations

- focus your energy on catching them being good

- look for ways to reinforce them

- reward the child in a way he or she likes

- all children are different -- use what works

- be consistent

- make it to the child's benefit to behave

Many parents object to the use of reward systems when it comes to reinforcing good behavior. They say, "I'm not going to bribe my child to behave. They should do it anyway." I respond that the definition of a bribe is to give someone something of value to encourage them to do something illegal. Behaving is not illegal! Generally, adults would not go to work if there was not some sort of payoff. It is important to think that children also work for goals and payoffs that turn them on. For difficult kids it is often necessary to set up a token system or a point system to help keep them on track.

Here is a simple 5-step "point or chip" system that has worked well for hundreds of parents.

1. Choose

- 3 chores -- dishes, cleaning their room, vacuuming, feeding the animals, etc. and

- 3 behaviors -- treating their sister well, getting ready for school on time, doing what mom and dad say the first time, etc.)

2. Assign a point (or poker chip) value to each chore and behavior, depending on how difficult each is for the child to accomplish. If the child has a lot of trouble doing something make it worth more points or chips than something he can do easily. Add up the possible points or chips the child can get each day if he

or she has a perfect day. Also, let the child know that he or she can earn bonus points or chips for especially cooperative and pleasant behavior. Tell the child that points or chips will only be given for chores and behaviors done on the first request. If you have to repeat yourself, the child will not get any points or chips.

3. Establish 2 lists of rewards:

- one for future incentives the child wishes to work for (toy, having a friend spend the night, special trip to restaurant or arcade, renting a video, etc.)

- another list for every day rewards (watching TV, playing with friends, playing video games, staying up an extra half hour, etc.)

4. Determine the point value necessary to redeem each reward.

About half should be spent on every day rewards. This allows a child if they have a really good day to save about half of their points or chips for special rewards down the line.

5. Every day add up the points and allow the child to use their rewards to buy every day privileges and keep a "savings account" for them for the points or chips they are able to save up to be used later on. This works to teach them the value and need for saving.

Notes:

- Initially make the system very reinforcing so that children will want to participate. Then slowly tighten the reigns on it as their behavior improves.

- You can use the rewards for almost any behavior you like.

- Reward as quickly as possible.
- Do not give chips or points away before the actual behavior or chore is done. In this system there is no credit!

Point systems are generally short lived because parents find it too hard to keep up with. They are best used when you have a specific habit or problem you are struggling with. It is critical to have an overall positive and reinforcing attitude toward your child.

Chapter Fourteen

GIVING CLEAR, QUICK,
UNEMOTIONAL CONSEQUENCES
(Or how to get your child to mind the first time, honestly)

In order for consequences to be effective they must be used with the other aspects of this program, i.e., goals, good parent-child relationship, clear expectations, positive reinforcement. Consequences by themselves change nothing, but when used in conjunction with the other aspects of the program they are very powerful in helping you parent children effectively.

I once saw an interaction between a mother and her 4-year-old son in a grocery store that turned my stomach. After the child ran off for the third time the mother jerked him by the arm, picked him off the ground and whacked him so hard his little body flew into the air. She then slammed him down into the cart and said, "You little brat, do what I say!" With a panicked look, he held his little arms up to hug her, at which point she turned and looked away from him. He then started to cry.

Too often, parents punish their children as a reaction to the anger they feel inside when they are out of control of themselves. This type of punishment causes the child to feel frightened, insecure and angry. When parents overreact they often feel guilty and frustrated.

It's important to distinguish between punishment and discipline. Punishment means to inflict a penalty for a wrong doing. Discipline, from the Greek root word disciple, means to teach or train. It's critical that we use discipline to teach children how to behave, rather than inflict punishment when they're not within acceptable boundaries.

As I mentioned in the last chapter, reinforcing good behavior is a much more effective change agent than giving consequences to bad behavior. Yet, there still are times when consequences are needed. Remember the metaphor of boundaries. When a child's behavior is outside the realm of the boundaries (acceptable behavior) it's important to have a way to nudge their behavior back in.

Here are eight components of effective discipline:

1. A good relationship with a child is a prerequisite to effective discipline.
When parents have a good relationship with a child, almost any form of discipline is effective. When the relationship is poor, however, almost no form of discipline works well. Never discipline a child in a way that damages your relationship with him or her.

2. You must be in control of yourself.
If you feel like you're going to explode, take a time out: take several deep breaths, count to fifty, hit a pillow, take a walk, call a friend, do anything to avoid exploding at the child. It's impossible to discipline effectively when you're out of control. It does more harm than good.

3. DON'T YELL, NAG OR BELITTLE.
What happens inside you when someone yells, nags or belittles you? If you're like me you immediately turn them off. These are very ineffective ways of behaving. They harm the situation more than help. Also, remember as I wrote before, there are some kids who get unconsciously "turned on" by turmoil. When you feel like yelling, talk softly (the difference in your behavior will frighten them).

4. Have a goal in mind for the behavior you're trying to change.
For the mother above, the goal was to get the child to stay near her. She would be more effective if she gave him a lot of positive attention for the time he stays near her, rather than giving him a lot of negative attention for when he goes away. By thinking in a positive way about the behaviors you would like the child to change, you're more likely to be helpful to him or her.

5. Develop a plan for discipline before you're actually in the situation.
This also prevents you from overreacting. Discipline should be as immediate as possible and should be a reminder to the child on how to change his or her behavior, not an assault. I often recommend a short time out method for younger children and a little bit longer one for older children. Parents can also have their children write lines or essays on how they'll change their behavior.

6. Whenever possible, use NATURAL and LOGICAL consequences. Ask yourself, "What's the natural or logical consequence to the misbehavior?" If the child refuses to do his homework, then he goes to school without it. If she is acting up at dinner so that she is put in a time out for 10 minutes, then she doesn't get to finish dinner if everyone else is done. If he refuses to put away his toys, then it is logical that the toys will be taken away for several days. Using these natural or logical consequences help children learn cause and effect and teaches them that they are responsible for their behavior.

7. Attitude is everything. Many parents ask my opinion on spanking. I generally tell them that whether or not you spank a child has nothing to do with effective discipline. How you discipline, not the method, is what's important. When you mildly spank a child when you're in control of yourself, for a specific "stated" reason, on the buttocks, and afterwards you give the child a hug, the spanking can be very effective. However, most parents don't use it that way. They spank a child when they're angry and on the verge of being out of control themselves. Use discipline for teaching. You and your child will both feel better.

8. Never withhold love, affection or time from a child who has misbehaved. When children are in trouble they need you the most. Let them know it's their behavior you're disciplining, but you still love them very much.

A TIME OUT METHOD THAT WORKS

When used properly, TIME OUT is an extremely effective discipline technique for children 2 to 12 years of age. Use following guidelines:

1. Give clear commands (outlined before). For example, "Antony take out the trash now." And then count to ten seconds to yourself. If you count out loud you teach the child to cue off your voice.

2. Expect immediate compliance. We teach our kids when to respond to us. When we repeat ourselves ten times and then get serious with a child we're teaching them not to listen to us until the tenth time we say something. Expect your child to obey you the first time you say something. When they do comply, notice and appreciate them. In our example, "Thanks Antony, I really like it when you do what I say the first time."

3. When the child doesn't comply, warn them only once and give them the choice to comply. In our case, "Antony, I told you to take out the trash now (spoken in a firm, but not hostile tone). You have a choice. You can take it out now or your can spend 10 minutes in time out and then you can do it. It's up to you."

4. If the child still doesn't comply IMMEDIATELY put them in TIME OUT! No bargaining, pleading, crying or cajoling gets them out of it at this point.

5. In my opinion, TIME OUTs are best served in a neutral, boring corner of the house. Don't use the child's bedroom because you have probably gone to great lengths and expense to make their bedroom a nice place to be. I like to use a TIME OUT chair, because there may be times when the child has to be in it for a while. Also, with a chair you can set the rule that in order for them to be in TIME OUT both of their buttocks need to be on the seat of the chair.

6. The time in TIME OUT should be their age in minutes or twice their age in minutes for more severe offenses. For example, if the child is 5 their TIME OUT should be five minutes long or ten minutes if it was a particularly bad offense. It's often good to get a timer to clearly set the time.

7. Their time starts when they are quiet. Children should not be allowed to badger you when they are in TIME OUT. It is a time for them to think about their behavior. They can't think about it when their mouths are going! If they start to cry, whine or nag you, simply reset the timer. Say very little, difficult kids may try to engage you in a fight but don't take the bait. I teach many parents to become a "broken record" when their child tries to engage them in a discussion during TIME OUT. Whenever they say something to you say, "Your time starts when you're quiet." If they persist, you persist (in a quiet soft tone), "Your time starts when you are quiet." After several times of this "broken record" they'll get the idea you are not going to respond to them.

8. Don't give in to their protests about being in TIME OUT. The first few times you use this method your child may become extremely upset. Expect it. But KNOW you're going to follow through! In unusual situations children may cry, fight or whine for several hours. They believe if they irritate you enough then you'll give in to their tantrum. Whatever you do, do your best to hang in there and not give in to the tantrum. Simply repeat to them, "Your time starts when you are quiet," and nothing else. If you go for 2 hours the first time and hold firm, it's likely the next time will be only an hour, then a half hour, then pretty soon the child will go to TIME OUT without a fuss. The first time you use TIME OUT don't do it when you're in a hurry to go somewhere. Be sure to leave yourself enough time to be able to do it right.

9. If the child refuses to stay in TIME OUT you have several choices. You can tell the child that he or she will get two spankings on their buttocks if they get out (make sure you're in control of your self before you use this method).

You can take away points or chips if they are on a token system.
You can ground them from activities they enjoy.

10. In order for the child to get out of TIME OUT, he or she must promise to do the thing they were asked to do and apologize for not doing it the first time they were asked. If they refuse to do it, they remain in TIME OUT until they do. It's very important to give the child the message that you're SERIOUS and that you MEAN what you say! If they can't do it or they broke a rule such as "no hitting" they must promise not to do it again. The apology they give you must be sincere. It's important that we teach children the value of "conscience" and feeling sorry when they do things that are wrong.

11. If the child has siblings who bother or tease them when they're in TIME OUT, make the sibling take their place. This is a very effective technique in keeping the others kids from further inflaming the situation.

For teenagers it is more effective and less humiliating to use "response cost" methods. When they break a rule or fail to comply that negative "response" costs them something important to them, such as privileges, money, phone time, going out on the weekends, etc. Make sure the consequence fits the crime. I've treated some teenagers who were grounded for the summer. By July they became depressed.

Since the **GUILT CYCLE** is so important to break I am repeating here from an earlier chapter to make sure you eliminate this from your parenting interaction.

GET RID OF GUILT

Perhaps the biggest roadblock to effective discipline is GUILT. Too often parents allow guilt to get in their way and render them totally ineffective in dealing with the difficult child.

Here is the **GUILT CYCLE** that often perpetuates bad behavior.

PARENT EXPLODES
(because they can't take the bad behavior any more)

PARENT FEELS GUILT
(because they overreacted or were excessively harsh)

PARENT ALLOWS THE CHILD TO GET AWAY WITH MISBEHAVIOR
(because of their guilt over the explosion toward the child)

PARENT FEELS TENSION BUILDING UP
(because they are not effectively dealing with the misbehavior)

PARENT EXPLODES
(and the cycle starts all over again)

It's very important when dealing with a child to break the guilt cycle. The best way to do this is by dealing with difficult behavior whenever it occurs and not allowing the tension to build up in you to the point where you explode. When you use the TIME OUT method I described above, you are disciplining the child almost immediately after they have misbehaved. At that point you are still in control of yourself and able to deal with them effectively. If you have told them to do something fifteen times or, because of guilt, allowed them to get away with misbehavior all day the chances are very high that you're going to explode.

Make Discipline a time for teaching and reshaping behavior.

Chapter Fifteen

HOW TO MANAGE PUBLIC MISBEHAVIOR EFFECTIVELY
(at the store, grandma's, restaurants and church)

When you're in public where do your kids misbehave?

In the car?

At church?

In the grocery store?

At the mall?

In restaurants?

At a friends house?

Or worse yet, at grandma's house?

One of the reasons children misbehave in public is because you've taught them that you're too embarrassed to deal with them effectively. Here's where we make them rethink their assumptions.

By using these simple principles, it really is possible to gain a measure of control over these situations and dramatically improve their behavior in public. Here's what you do:

1. Before you go somewhere give the child a set of simple rules.

For example, if you're going to the store tell the child

"Stay close,
 don't beg and
 don't touch."

Then have the child repeat these rules back to you and have him or her promise to follow them!

2. Set up a reward system for when the child complies. Tell them specifically if they follow the rules that they will get a reward (a pack of sugarless gum, their favorite cereal, extra points, etc.). The fact is that most of the time we go to the store we allow the child to get "a little something" anyway. Now we're making them work for it.

3. Set up clear consequences if they break the rules AND FOLLOW THROUGH WITH THEM! Children must learn that you mean what you say and that you're willing to back it up even if it is at grandma's house. When they think they can get their way they generally attempt it. Some examples of consequences in public include time out in the store or at a friends house, going to the car, taking away points or privileges.

4. Set up specific training periods to improve specifically the child's behavior in public. Several years ago, I took my youngest daughter shopping for school shoes. Before we went into the store I had given her the rules (stay close, don't beg, be cooperative) and I had her repeat them back to me. In the shoe department of Mervyn's she didn't cooperate by trying on any pairs of shoes I thought looked nice (maybe I have terrible taste) and only wanted a pair of shoes that were not appropriate for school. When I told her no and reminded her about the rule to cooperate she said, "I don't care. You are going to buy me the shoes I want!" My eyes got big and I said, "Excuse me, Kaitlyn." "You heard me," she said, "I want these shoes." Right there in Mervyn's Kaitlyn went in time out. For 7 minutes (she was seven at the time) she had her nose up against a blank wall, with the shoe salesman and other customers looking on. One person even asked me why I was so cruel to my daughter. I told him to stay out of my duty to parent my child. After she served her time I gave her a hug and she apologized. Then we tried on appropriate shoes. I believe that it is important to not allow her to talk to me that way (better to get these attitudes before they turn 14!) and you have more influence.

Managing public misbehavior works if you follow these simple steps! Do it every time you go somewhere and you'll notice a marked difference in your ability to go in public with your child.

Chapter Sixteen

FIVE CRITICAL MISTAKES
PARENTS MAKE WITH TEENAGERS

Mini-Diagnostic Quiz

HOW'S YOUR RELATIONSHIP WITH YOUR TEENAGER?

Check off the statements which apply to you

___ 1. Do you find yourself giving your children the same lectures your parents gave you?

___ 2. Do your feelings get hurt when your teenager wants to spend more and more time with his or her friends?

___ 3. In dealing with your children do you have a tendency to forget what it was like for you when you were their age?

___ 4. Do you do more lecturing than listening to your teenager?

___ 5. Are you unable to set firm limits with your teenager?

___ 6. Do you have a tendency to be overcontrolling with your children rather than give them reasonable choices (about clothes, music, friends, etc.)

___ 7. Do you argue with your teenager in an attempt to get them to think your way?

___ 8. Do you feel bullied by your teenager?

___ 9. Does your teenager avoid talking to you about sensitive issues (i.e., sex and drugs)?

Total number of statements checked: ___

0 - 1: Your relationship with your teenager is likely to be mutually satisfying and effective

2 - 4: Like most parents, you're doing some things right and you have some important areas to work on

5 - 9: There is probably a need to look further into how you can improve your relationship with your teenager

Parenting teenagers is one of the most difficult tasks known to Man. Few other challenges simultaneously deal with acne, raging hormones, peer groups, first dates and driver's education. If you have doubts about the difficulty of raising a teenager, take a minute to reflect upon the difficulties you put your parents through when you were a teen.

Though many of us have said we'll do things differently from our parents, most of us find that we act just like them. Parenting is often automatic. It's this automatic or reflexive nature that often causes trouble between parents and teens.

Of course, as parents, we all make mistakes. Most of them are insignificant and don't amount to much. However some mistakes parents make with teenagers really do matter and can cause problems for years to come. In my experience as a psychiatrist I have noticed five critical mistakes parents make with teenagers. If you can avoid them, you'll probably save yourself years of what you put your parents through.

1. Failure to Understand Normal Development

It is critical in raising teenagers to understand what is normal at different ages. The two main psychological tasks of adolescence are developing a sense of identity ("Who am I?") and a sense of independence ("Can I make some of my own decisions?"). Identity is formed, in part, from a teenager's peer group, which normally becomes more important during this time. Independence often rears its head in the form of rebelliousness and/or questioning the authority and values of the parents. Many parents don't understand this behavior as normal and become critical of the teenager's attitude. Many parents also feel rejected by the teenager. When a child is 8 years old the parents are often idolized. The child wants to spend as much time as possible with the parents. When the child is 13 or 14, he or she wants to spend more and more time with friends. Many parents take this new attitude as rejection and feel hurt. In turn, these parents may reject the child by spending more time at work or with the other children. This is a mistake. When a normal adolescent child pulls away, it's done for developmental reasons, not for rejection. When they feel their parents pull away, the child feels rejected and confused. Of course, they would never say so, but it becomes evident in their behavior. Parental involvement is critical to a teenager's healthy development.

2. Failure to Remember Your Own Adolescence

One of the best ways to help a teenager through adolescence is for you to remember what it was like to be a teenager. If you can develop empathy for what it's like to go through puberty, acne, first dates, and high school English, then you're likely to be helpful to your teen. If you block out your teenage years (and many of us have good reason to) then it'll be easy for you to give your child the same lecture your parents gave you about "how good you have it," and how "you need to change your attitude."

3. Failure to Listen

Listening to kids is the key to teaching them about solving problems. Whenever my teenagers come to me with a problem I have many solutions for them. What I have learned is they don't need my solutions, they need me to listen so that they can talk through the situation. When they are able to do this they feel much better about themselves, and they are much more invested in the solution. As parents, we must restrain our tendency to tell kids how to solve their problems. We can give them ideas or share what it was like for us when we encountered a similar problem, but what works best is to listen.

4. Failure to Set Reasonable Limits

Limit setting is another key to raising healthy teenagers. Reasonable limits and clear expectations are a must for teenagers. Many parents feel helpless and bullied by their teenagers' demands, often giving in to unreasonable curfews or dress standards just to avoid an argument. This is especially true for parents who were raised in overly strict homes and are now trying to do everything opposite from their own parents. Parents have a right and a responsibility to be in control, to set limits, and to expect the teenager to pull his or her fair share at home. Abdicating responsibility to avoid hassles leads to greater trouble down the road.

5. Failure to Give Choices

Setting reasonable limits, however, does not mean making all the decisions for a teenager. Teenagers need to have choices. Self-esteem and independence are enhanced when they feel they can make good decisions for themselves. The more "supervised" decisions teenagers can make for themselves, the greater competence they'll have to make good independent decisions in the future. Making all the decisions for children breeds dependence and a sense of inadequacy. Let them make as many decisions as they are able to do under your guidance and within the reasonable limits you set.

Avoiding these five mistakes with teenagers will help both parents and their teenagers get through difficult and challenging times.

Chapter Seventeen

DEALING WITH AGGRESSIVE BEHAVIOR IN CHILDREN AND TEENS

Aggressiveness in children and teenagers is frightening to parents. Many parents fear it foretells violent or antisocial behavior later on. It is critical to understand and deal with this type of behavior early.

The reasons behind aggressiveness in children and teenagers may be many. Here are some of the common ones:

Re-enacting events seen. Children from violent homes have a tendency to use aggressiveness as a means to get their way, or as a reflex to a tense situation. When a child sees their father hit their mother they receive an unconscious message about that being normal behavior.

Victim of abuse (verbal, physical, sexual or emotional). Children who are or have been abused lose their sense of bonding and boundaries. They have a higher tendency to strike out when they're frustrated because that's what others did to them.

Significant stress in the home or at school. Generally, children have their breaking point at a lower level than adults. Stress in the home (alcoholic parent, divorce, family financial problems, health problems, etc.) may bring out aggressive tendencies in children. Understanding their environment is critical to understanding aggressiveness.

Mental illness. As environmental stress can bring on aggressiveness, so can internal stress or pressure. Depression, manic-depression, anxiety, psychosis and other mental disorders can impair the child's ability to think to the point where they become violent. I once treated a child who saw enormous monsters that he would strike out at to protect himself. Likewise, children with Attention Deficit Disorder are impulsive and often aggressive.

Alcohol or other drug abuse. I have treated kids as young as nine years old for substance abuse. Drug intoxication or withdrawal can cause significantly violent or erratic behavior. PCP laced marijuana and inhalants seem to be the worst culprits. In this era, it's important think of alcohol or drug abuse no matter the age of violent behavior.

Brain trauma, minor or major. Many people, including some doctors, do not understand the serious effects caused by head injuries. Studies have shown that up to 70% of people with minor head injuries (brief loss of consciousness) have impaired memories and are irritable. In my experience this is especially true if the injury is on the left side.

Here are several guidelines in dealing with an aggressive child:

Start early. When small children show signs of aggressive behavior this is the best place to intervene with clear expectations, firm limits, and lots of positive rewards for non-aggressive play and behavior.

Clear expectations. It is important to provide clear guidelines as to what is acceptable and what is not. Unfortunately, many parents of aggressive kids walk the fence and tell the child that it is OK to defend themselves with force if they feel attacked. These kids then use self-defense as a way to explain fights they provoke. If a child has a tendency toward violence it's important to tell him or her that no violence will be tolerated. It takes the smarter person to learn how to walk away from a fight.

Reward non-violent behavior as much as possible. Try to catch the child acting appropriately, at home with his or her friends, and at school. Positive reinforcement is more effective than discipline.

Quick, clear, unemotional and non-violent consequences. Don't fight violence with violence. It is important for parents to have a plan when aggressiveness appears. Isolation is often the best technique (time out, grounding, withholding privileges, etc.)

Teach the child relaxation techniques. Teaching aggressive children to control their outbursts may be easier than you think. In my office I teach aggressive children to take control of their breathing pattern, which often increases dramatically before they lose control. By teaching them how to slow down their breathing rate it gives a child a sense of internal control. They become better able to be in touch with the warning signs their body might give alerting them that the situation is getting out of control.

Give the child alternatives. When a child is frequently in trouble for aggressiveness they may not know their options when faced with a difficult situation. My patients develop a list of "10 things to do when I get mad." They put this list up someplace where they can read it every day.

Medical evaluation by a specialist. If the above guidelines are not effective it is necessary to have the child evaluated by either a child neurologist or a child psychiatrist. These physicians may be able to help find out if there is any physical cause for the problem. They often order EEG or blood flow studies to help understand the patterns in the brain.

Medications may help. In the last decade there have been several medications that have proven valuable in the treatment of aggressiveness, including blood pressure and anti-seizure medications.

The main point of this chapter is that if you have a child or teenager who has a tendency toward aggressiveness you need to deal with the problem as early as possible. Early intervention is likely to be more helpful. It is also helpful to see this problem as a "problem to be solved," rather than a statement on the child's personality, character or adult life.

Chapter Eighteen

TURNING MISTAKES INTO POSITIVE LESSONS

What happened when you made a mistake as a child? When you spilled something at the dinner table or you did poorly on a test? Were you berated and yelled at for the mistake or were you encouraged to learn something from it?

One of the most critical lessons a parent can teach a difficult child is how to learn from mistakes. Too often as parents we are super critical of ourselves when we fail which then transfers to how we treat our children when they fail at something.

In order to help our children feel good about themselves we must help them be competent, which is even more difficult for kids who have problems. Of course, competent people make mistakes, the difference is that they have the ability to learn from them and move on to other things rather than to beat themselves up for it.

For example, think about the 4-year-old child who spills orange juice at breakfast. Many parents, who are in a hurry to get off to work, get stressed by the delay in schedule and take their frustration out by yelling at the child. The child feels incompetent and the next time the child tries to pour juice he'll feel anxious and tense, remembering his recent failure -- this makes him more likely to spill it again.

In the parenting groups I teach, I have parents focus their energy on helping their child learn from the mistakes they make. So instead of yelling at the child for the spilled orange juice, I recommend that a parent teach the child how to clean up the mess and then take him over to the sink and have him pour 10 glasses of orange juice. In that way, he's gone from making a mistake to learning 2 skills -- cleaning up a mess and pouring juice. He's gone from feeling clumsy and stupid to feeling competent.

After I gave that particular class, one of the parents had an incident the following week where her 3-year-old spilled her milk at the table. As the little girl cowered the mother's first instinct was to get angry. She remembered what I said, however, and tried the new approach. She taught her daughter to clean up the milk and then had her pour 10 glasses of milk over the sink. She reported that interaction with her daughter turned into something very special, where they laughed and learned together, and the mother said that she had never felt better as a parent. Helping children to be competent is a real turn on for almost all parents.

Here are 5 principles to guide you in helping your children learn from their mistakes:

1. You need to be able to learn from your mistakes. It's very hard to teach someone something you don't do yourself. If you have a tendency to be harsh and self-critical when you make a mistake, your kids will pick up the message that it's not OK to fail. Teach by example.

2. Don't overreact or criticize mistakes. Kids (and adults) do not learn well when they're stressed -- teach them in a relaxing and positive atmosphere. This allows children to understand that we all make mistakes and it's more helpful if we can learn from them.

3. Talk about some of the times when you messed up. By becoming human and being honest with your kids they'll be able to relate to you. Amazingly, many children think that their parents are perfect, and that they can never live up to them. Be honest with your children about the mistakes you've made and your children will become more tolerant of themselves.

4. After a mistake, ask the child what he or she could do differently the next time. Watch your tone of voice. You can be condescending, which is not helpful, or you can be interested in what ideas the child might have for changing things the next time. Being interested is a strong way to let a child know that you approve of what they're trying to do.

5. Give the child a simple method for solving problems. Include such things as looking at all the options, gathering more information from people who are likely to know, weighing the risks and the benefits of certain actions and choosing from among the alternatives. Teaching children a method for solving problems gives them a framework to work from when they're feeling overwhelmed. It's my opinion that many children and teenagers become depressed and suicidal because they are poor problem solvers and they emotionally beat themselves up when they make a mistake. These children lose hope that they can solve the difficult problems in their lives so they give up.

In order to raise healthy children it is critical to teach them how to learn from the mistakes they make and to give them a framework for problem solving.

Chapter Nineteen

CHARACTERISTICS OF RESILIENT PEOPLE

Several years ago I met Jim, a very special 18 year old. He was different than the majority of teenagers I see at the hospital or in my office. Jim was responsible, considerate, kind, energetic and self-sufficient. What is particularly interesting about Jim is that, like many of my patients, he had a persistently difficult childhood. His parents divorced when he was very young. They could never get along with each other and they often fought custody battles over Jim, placing him in the middle. He had multiple moves and he was constantly changing schools and changing friends.

Jim had plenty of excuses to have a lousy life. In fact many psychiatrists would conclude that such a childhood would damage a child for life. Yet, Jim took responsibility for his life, despite the social difficulties he faced. He earned a 3.62 grade point average in high school, worked after school and was involved in volunteer organizations that went into elementary schools to teach youngsters how to stay away from drugs.

What's the difference between Jim and those people who have difficult lives and turn to drugs or other self-destructive behaviors? What accounts for Jim's resilience? Over the past several years behavioral scientists have started to research people like Jim to understand how people remain healthy, rather than just focusing on how people become ill. Resilient people tend to have five characteristics in common.

First, and most important, these people have an inner sense of personal responsibility. They take charge of their lives and do not blame other people for their problems. Jim could have easily blamed his parents' inability to get along or his multiple moves on why he didn't accomplish his goals, but he didn't. He knew that if he wanted to achieve something it was up to him to make it happen.

Second, resilient people have a sense of purpose and they are focused on goals that are important to them. Often these people focus on helping others. Jim was clear on his academic goals and he also derived pleasure from teaching children how to stay away from drugs. His life had meaning that shielded him from some of life's pain.

Third, another hallmark of resilient people is that they are able to learn from their mistakes. They have as many or more problems and hardships as others, but they handle their mistakes in a different way. Instead of beating themselves up for mistakes or medicating their pain with drugs or alcohol they try hard to learn something from their failures. Jim could have easily hated both of his parents for putting him through the difficult times, yet he nurtured the relationship with both of his parents. In talking with him, he told me he learned a lot about what not to do in a divorce and he gained tremendous empathy for other kids who went through hard times.

Fourth, healthy, resilient people also surround themselves with positive people. They find friends who support and help them and stay away from people who put them down. Jim and his friends had similar goals and values which made it easier for Jim to stay on track. At any age, peer group is very important.

Fifth, these people talk to themselves in a positive and supportive way. They are much more aware of their own reactions and tend not to react toward situations before they take time to evaluate them. I call this "conscious living," which means you're able to match your behavior to the goals you've set for your life.

Jim is a very special person. It's so important for scientists to study more people like him so that we can focus our efforts on developing healthy kids rather than just teaching them how to avoid the pitfalls of life.

Chapter Twenty

PREVENTING EATING DISORDERS IN KIDS

Many parents are frustrated over the eating habits of their children. They complain that all their kids want to eat is junk food or that meal times are frequently tense where they engage in repetitive battles over food. Parents often find themselves saying, "Eat this. Try that. Eat your vegetables. Try a little bit more. You can't leave the table until you clean your plate!" The child often responds, "No! I don't like it. It'll make me throw up! I'm full (after two bites). I want something else." Everyone at the table feels upset and no one enjoys eating together.

Unfortunately, I've had personal experience with these "dinner time wars." When our oldest son was a toddler we engaged in the same kind of destructive behavior. Meal time was a struggle and it affected everyone's mood for the rest of the evening. My wife would get angry with him if he didn't eat all of his dinner and they engaged in recurrent battles that made me not want to come home for dinner. In wanting to support my wife, I reluctantly got after him as well. These battles were really confusing to me. When I was growing up with a brother and 5 sisters, if you didn't eat it was too bad, someone else would get the goods. My wife, on the other hand, was forced to eat everything on her plate when she was a child. Dinner time could go on for hours. She once told me how she would hide her peas in her napkin and feed them to her dog when her parents weren't looking. Ah ha! Conflicts in the past breed problems in future generations.

During my child psychiatry training, however, one of my supervisors helped us out of the struggle. She told us that our son wasn't going to starve to death. He was going through a normal oppositional period and that if we continued to struggle around food that he may end up with some form of an eating disorder. She recommended the following rules around mealtime to help children develop healthy habits:

1. The parents decide what's for meals, with liberal input from the child.

2. A child should decide how much or how little he or she eats from their plate.

3. If the child is a picky eater only put a small portion of food on their plate.

4. If the child does not eat at all there should be no arrangements made for a "special menu." Also, if the child refuses to eat he or she cannot have sweets for deserts but may have some fruit or other healthy snack.

5. Keep mainly healthy food in the house.

The basic message was get out of the struggle around food! To our amazement, when we followed her rules and allowed our son to control how much or how little he ate at mealtime there were no more struggles around food. He actually gained weight and mealtime became a more special family time.

Clinically, I've found that prolonged parent-child struggles around food significantly increase the risk for eating problems. In fact, there is a serious epidemic of obesity in our culture. Over the past 15 years there has also been a dramatic rise in the eating disorders of teenage obesity, anorexia nervosa (self-starvation) and bulimia (bingeing and purging behaviors). One clear way of preventing these problems is to give the child as much control as is reasonable over what and how much they eat. If they have a tendency to eat a lot of sweets, don't keep a lot of them around the house. Buy more fruit and vegetables (such as carrots and celery) to snack on. When a child is hungry he or she will eat what's there.

Another hint is to not use food as a way of soothing babies and children who are upset. This only teaches them to use food later in life to comfort them when they're anxious or unhappy, which increases the risk for obesity.

Mealtime can be a special time with prayers, lively discussions, joking and sharing. Do everything you can to get out of food struggles and keep it special.

Chapter Twenty One

CHOICES AND SUPERVISION

The concepts of "giving children choices" and "supervision" are central to good parenting, especially with difficult kids.

CHOICES

Many parents don't understand that children need to have choices in their life if they are going to learn how to make good decisions. Some parents erroneously believe that if they make all of the decisions for their children then they are protecting and loving their child. These parents tell their children what they are going to wear, what they'll eat, who their friends will be, and what course of study to pursue in school.

Often, the children are not so appreciative of this much guidance. In fact, when parents are overcontrolling that often breeds oppositional children who oppose even those suggestions that are clearly in their best interest. These kids fight their parents on every decision and the turmoil in a family increases (actually the opposite response that the parent intended).

Sometimes, more dependent children welcome the fact that their parents make all the decisions for them. They feel so insecure about themselves and feel that their parents will do a better job. Unfortunately, parental overcontrol with these children breeds kids who are unwilling to make decisions on their own and who are likely to follow the crowd, maybe into premature sex and drugs.

The best approach with kids is something I call "Supervised Independent Choices" (SIC). SIC allows a child to choose from a wide range of options within boundaries that are acceptable to the family's values. Here are some examples:

** Clothing: Many parents battle with their children over clothes, especially when the parents say, "Put this on!" Children will be much more cooperative if they have a range of clothes to pick from. It is better, for example, on a school morning to say, "Which of these outfits would you like to wear," (giving a choice of 3 or 4 outfits) rather than, "Put this outfit on."

** Food: Allowing children to choose between available healthy foods will encourage good eating habits and prevent some of the struggles around food that sometimes lead to eating disorders. It's often good for parents to ask children what they like and work those foods into the family diet. Note: SIC means choosing between what is acceptable, significant amounts of junk food should not be acceptable.

** Hairstyles: Again, allowing some leeway and choice is essential. Hairstyle is often a sign of individuality. It's important to give the child or teen some room within the boundaries that are acceptable to you.

** Friends: This is a tricky area. Friends have a huge influence on how children and teenagers behave and also on how they perceive the world. If they spend time with children who are motivated and respectful, odds are that will rub off on them. If they spend time with kids who are disrespectful and selfish those attitudes will infect them as well. The best way to approach this area is to get your child involved with activities with other kids who have parents who care. Organized athletics, scouting, musical groups, etc., are examples of activities that have high parent involvement. If you are too pushy though in choosing your children's friends they may go the opposite way. I once treated a teenage girl who was dating a boy of a different race. This drove her father crazy, because he was a racially prejudiced man. After getting to know the girl it was clear she was dating this person to get her father upset. I told the dad to back off on complaining about the other person and work on his relationship with his daughter. Several months after the father did this she stopped dating this other person.

In a similar way, don't tell teenagers what they can and cannot do! When I turned 18 years old I had to sign up for the draft. The Vietnam War was in high gear and all 18 year old men had to register with their local draft boards. While I was at the draft board I met with a recruiter who told me about US Army programs. At the time I wanted to be a veterinarian and the recruiter told me about a program the Army had to be a veterinarian's assistant. Slightly intrigued by the idea, I went home and told my father that I was thinking about joining the Army to get the training. He said, "Danny, you can't go into the Army." I said, "I'm 18. I can do whatever I want!" Before I saw this recruiter I had no intention of joining the military. I wasn't that excited about war and some of my friends had died in Vietnam. But now that my father said that it was something I couldn't do, I had to do it! Within 3 weeks I was at Fort Ord in basic training, hating every minute of it. Looking back on my life, going into the military was one of the best things that happened to me, but if you want to have influence on your teenagers don't tell them what they can and cannot do, unless it involves drugs.

NO CHOICE

** Drugs, alcohol and smoking: This is an area where there should be no choices. Drugs, alcohol and smoking are uniformly bad for children and teens and parents need to let kids know that there is no room for negotiation. Smoking seems to be the catalyst for alcohol and drug abuse. Seventy percent of the teenagers who smoke also use others drugs. Only two percent of the kids who don't smoke use other drugs. If you as a parent smoke you're setting a terrible example for your kids, because kids generally do what you do not what you say!

SUPERVISION

Difficult kids tell you by their behavior that they're in need of supervision. Even though many kids and teens complain about too much supervision, they feel that you don't care when you don't supervise them. It is essential with difficult kids (up to the age of 16 or 17) to know:

where they are,
who they are with and
what they are doing.

Several research studies have shown that the kids who get into the most trouble are those kids who are not properly supervised. "Trust but verify" is a good phrase to keep in mind with difficult kids. When they know you're going to check to see if they are where they said they would be they are more likely than not to be there.

If you want your children to choose your values in life work on your relationship with them! The children who are counterculture (and often a huge embarrassment to their parents), in my experience, are basically telling their parents off. Relationship is central.

Chapter Twenty Two

THOUGHTS ON TELEVISION, VIDEO GAMES AND THE INTERNET

In our mobile society, with a lack of extended family support and where both parents usually work outside the home, parents have needed to find prolonged daycare and babysitter situations for their children. This is particularly true for difficult children, who often go through day care providers, as they go through pairs of shoes. Many families in our society have found the answer to their babysitting problems: television, video games and Internet web browsing.

The amount of time that children and teenagers (and even adults) spend watching television, playing video games and surfing on the Internet has more than doubled over the past 30 years. On average, children spend much less time playing with friends and much more time playing with remote controls, joysticks and keyboards. There are several reasons why this trend is harmful to children, especially children and teens with ADD.

First, extended time watching television, playing video games or surfing on the Internet takes time away from social interactions. Children need social interactions in order to mature and to be able to relate to others as adults. Children who have difficulty in social situations are often happy to escape the painful interactions with others. Thus, they are less likely to learn the social skills they need to get along.

Two, watching television, playing video games, and net browsing are often passive, "no brain" activities. With television, everything is provided for the viewer, nothing is left to the imagination. The mind is a passive recipient of the action on the tube. Video games are only slightly different. Whenever a person plays a new game, they need to figure out strategy and use thinking skills to beat the game. That part is good. But most children and teens who play these games, do so on a repetitive basis. They play the same game, over, and over, and over. Thus, like television, it becomes a "no brain" activity. In EEG or brain wave studies that I have performed in my office, both television and video games are a "no brain" activity. These activities do not activate a person's brain; rather they cause a decrease in brain activity. The brain is like a muscle, the more that it is used, the stronger it becomes. The more time that it spends in passive activities, the weaker it becomes. There have been other studies in the past several years that have demonstrated that achievement and performance in school are inversely related to the amount of time spent watching television or playing video games. The more TV, video games, or net browsing, the worse the grades and performance scores in school.

Three, television and video games are not an appropriate place to learn values and problem solving skills. With the fast pace of society and the overall decline of religious values in the every -day lives of children and teens, television (and yes, even video games) has become a prime source of programming values.

Typical television values and messages include:

when you're angry, you can hit or shoot someone
  (violence is a very common way people solve problems on television),

the good life is depicted with lite beer and skinny women
  (encouraging alcohol use and eating disorders)

sexual promiscuity
  (as seen in three o'clock in the afternoon on MTV)

being sarcastic and rude is funny and acceptable family behavior
  (from All In The Family to the Simpsons and Married With Children) and

the world is a dangerous place to live
  (anyone who watches the evening news knows this).

Here are several family rules for watching television and playing video games to consider:

* limit the time per day of television, video games, and Internet surfing
  (no more than an hour total)

* supervise what they watch, the games they play and the web sites they visit

* discuss television scenes that impact on a child or teen's morals and values

* encourage more creative and productive activities for children and teens, where they use their minds.

Chapter Twenty Three

RAISING CHILDREN TOGETHER WHEN BOTH PARENTS WORK

Over the last thirty years there has been a dramatic increase in the number of two parent working families. This trend is not likely to change, especially with the high housing prices in our area and the societal expectations that women should have their own careers. This trend is combined with increased family mobility and the subsequent lack of nearby family members. Together, the result is that children are spending less and less time with their parents or relatives and more time with day care workers, or perhaps just by themselves as latch key kids.

I believe that these trends will have serious societal consequences if parents do not provide strong leadership to their children. Here are 10 guidelines for raising healthy children in two parent working families.

1. Time: Good parent-child relationships require time. Actual, physical time that is consistent and that the child can depend on. It doesn't have to be hours of time, but it's important to spend some time with children nearly every day. When you spend time with a child it's important to really be there with them. Keep distractions to a minimum and your attention on them. In today's fast paced life many parents let precious child-centered moments go. Guard against it. Time is the cornerstone of good parenting.

2. Be A Good Listener: When children know that you'll listen and really hear what they have to say, they are more willing to share their feelings and thoughts. When a parent puts down a child's idea or criticizes their words it causes a child to withdraw and rely more on their friends. If you want to have influence in your child's life be a good listener. They'll allow you to help them talk through their problems.

3. Set Clear Expectations: Letting a child know up front what you expect from him or her sets the tone for good behavior. Don't be afraid to expect your children to do chores and help around the house. Most kids will complain. Don't allow their grumbling to cause you to back off. When children participate in their care of a household their work ethic is improved and they generally feel more a part of the family.

4. Do Not Allow Guilt To Get In The Way: Many parents feel guilty for working long hours. Subsequently, they give in to their child's whining or allow bad behavior to go undisciplined. Good parents are firm. Guilt is counterproductive.

5. Do Not Substitute Money For Love Or Time: Teaching children to handle money is important, but don't use money as a substitute for your time or love. Given the materialistic messages television feeds children it's easy for them to gratify their temporary needs by buying something. Make them work for what they buy. If they earn it through work it will have value for them.

6. Consistency of Child Care: One of the most important psychological needs of a child is for a consistently firm and positive caregiver. The choice of a caregiver can help make working worry free for parents or it can cause endless grief. Take the time initially to find a situation that is stable and positive. Frequent care giver changes may be harmful for a child. It may be necessary to go the extra mile to keep a good person or situation for a child.

7. Supervision Is Key: The number of latch key kids in this country frightens me. Often kids left to themselves get into the most trouble. Research has demonstrated that delinquent children often come from homes where there was little or no supervision. Children are not born "knowing the ropes" of acceptable behavior. They need to be taught and then supervised. I think it's critical for parents to know where their children are, who they are with, and what they are doing. Children often complain about tight supervision, but unsupervised children often feel that their parents really don't care about them.

8. Notice More Positives Than Negatives: This is a very tough part of parenting. It's easy to notices kids when they irritate us. It's a lot harder to notice their good behavior. But if you want good behavior from your child you have to notice the things you like about them. When children feel ignored they subconsciously misbehave to make us pay attention to them. So, it's up to you: notice them when they're good, which takes effort, or notice them when they irritate you, which takes a lot out of you both.

9. Discipline Is For Teaching: Parents are more likely to lose control with children when they are tired. When both parents work outside the home there may be a tendency for them to be tired and irritable at the same time. This can spell trouble. Never discipline a child when you're out of control of yourself. Use discipline for teaching, not a way to ventilate anger.

10. Work On The Marriage: Children learn about relationships by watching their parents. Children also feel most secure when their parents are doing well as a couple. The best thing you can do for a child is to love your spouse.

Chapter Twenty Four

BEING A GOOD PARENT TO YOURSELF

Being a good parent to yourself is absolutely essential when you have a difficult child. Difficult kids take up so much time, energy and emotion that it is necessary for parents to take good care of themselves if they are to have the stamina required to deal with them effectively.

Carol, a 26-year-old mother of 2, was abandoned by her mother when she was 3 years old. She was subsequently raised partially by her father and by an orphanage. She often felt lonely even though there were always people around. In raising her own children, she was confused about what was good for them and had a difficult time disciplining them. Additionally, she was very self-critical and had trouble pushing herself to do things that were good for her. She often felt depressed.

In therapy with her over several months we came to the conclusion that she was missing a very important part of herself -- "the good mother." Since her mother had left her early on in life, she was never able to internalize the traits that a protective, nurturing, firm, and loving mother gives to her child. She lacked basic self-mothering skills.

In helping her to heal she has gone back in her mind to imagine the little girl inside of herself. She has begun to reparent herself. She asks herself, "What do little girls need?" And then she tries to give those things to herself. For example, she knows that good mothers are firm with their children. So when she has a task to complete, such as the laundry, she does not put it off anymore, she goes ahead and does it, which makes her feel a sense of relief and accomplishment.

Many people grew up in homes with parents who were overly critical, harsh, or neglectful. As such, a part of themselves have become critical, harsh, and neglectful. Those voices and feelings from the past continue to haunt them. How do you treat yourself? How do you treat the child within you? I think that many of us need to learn how to reparent the child within. Here are seven traits of a "good parent," see if they apply to how you treat yourself.

1. A "good parent" loves her children no matter what. She doesn't always like or approve of what they do, but she always loves them. Do you love yourself no matter what?

2. A "good parent" notices her children when they do things she likes. Her focus is on building self-esteem, rather than tearing it down. When was the last time you noticed something good about yourself?

3. A "good parent" is firm with her children and will push them to do things that are good for them, even if they do not want to do them. She pushes them to do it anyway. Are you good at pushing yourself (in a kind way) to do the things you need done?

4. A "good parent" wants her children to be independent and encourages her children to have choices and make decisions for themselves under her supervision. Do you feel good about yourself independently, or do you depend on the opinion of others to make yourself feel good?

5. A "good parent" helps her children learn from their mistakes. She does not berate them when they mess up, rather she helps them look at what happened and helps them figure out what to do differently the next time. Do you learn from your mistakes or just beat yourself up when you make them?

6. A "good parent" is not perfect. No one can relate to a perfect person and a good parent is someone who is easy to relate to. Do you expect yourself to be perfect and then beat yourself up when you're not?

7. A "good parent" always notices more good than bad in her children. What do you have a tendency notice about yourself -- good or bad?

When we grow up we become, in a sense, our own parents. How we treat ourselves plays a large role in what we get out of life.

Chapter Twenty Five

135 BEST THINGS YOU
CAN DO FOR YOUR CHILD

Few things are more important in life than raising children. Yet, most people receive no formal parent training or education. In large measure, parenting skills are developed by watching how our own parents dealt with us and our brothers and sisters. When we have relaxed and effective parents, our parenting skills tend to work. When our parents were less than skilled in dealing with children, we tend to have difficulty dealing with our own children.

Although parenting can be tremendously rewarding, it is often filled with heartache, confusion and pain. This little book is a crash course in superior parenting skills. If you follow the principles outlined here you will notice a marked increase in your effectiveness with your child, along with a more positive and fulfilling relationship.

No one can follow all of the suggestions listed. Choose the ones appropriate to your situation. These "best things you can do for your child" have been gathered over years of clinical experience with both "difficult" and "not-so-difficult" children and teenagers.

Remember What It Is Like To Be A Child

1. Remember what it is like to be a child (the good and the bad). Remember how you felt when you were their age. This will help you relate to their worries and concerns.

2. Remember how it felt when your mom or dad were too busy for you.

3. Remember what it felt like to tell a lie and how you wish your parents would have reacted when they found out.

4. Remember how you felt when your parents fought with each other (do you fight in the same way with your spouse?)

5. Remember how it felt when your mom or dad took you someplace special.

6. Remember meal times when you were a child. Were they a positive experience (and why) or were they a negative experience (and why)?

7. Remember how you felt at bedtime.

8. Remember the first time you asked someone out on a date, or were asked out, and the intense anxiety that goes along with dating.

9. Remember your sexual feelings and experiences as a child and teenager.

10. Remember the worst teachers you had, so that you can relate to them when they complain about school.

11. Remember the best teachers you had, so that you can tell your children how good school can be.

Develop Clear Goals For Yourself As A Parent And For Your Child

12. Develop clear, written goals for raising your children. Goals which spell out the kind of person you'd like them to become. Then review the goals every month to see if your behavior is encouraging what you want. In all of my interactions with my children I try to ask myself if my actions encourage the behaviors I want.

Goals For Yourself As A Parent (the overall goal is to be a competent and positive force in the child's life)

13. Be involved with your child. Ensure you have enough time with them so that you can influence their direction.

14. Be open with your child. Talk with them in such a way that will help them talk to you when they need to.

15. Be firm/set limits. Provide appropriate supervision and limits until they develop their own moral/internal controls.

16. Be together with their other parent in dealing with the child. Whether married or divorced, it is best when parents support each other in their interactions with a child.

17. Be kind. Raise your children in such a way so that they will want to come and see you after they leave home. Being a parent is also a selfish job.

18. Be fun. Joke, clown and play with your kids. Having fun is essential to both physical and emotional health.

Develop Clear Goals For Your Child (the overall goal is to enhance development)

19. Be relational. We live in a relational world. It is imperative that I teach my child how to get along with others.

20. Be responsible. My child needs to believe and act as if he or she has some control over his or her life; that when bad things happen it is not always someone else's fault. Otherwise, he or she will act like a victim and have no personal power in life.

21. Be independent. I will allow my child to have some choices over his or her own life. This will enable the child to be able to make good decisions on his or her own.

22. Be self-confident. I will encourage my child to be involved with different activities where he or she can feel a sense of competence. Self-confidence often comes from our ability to be able to master tasks and sports.

23. Be self-accepting. I will notice more positive than negative in my child. This will enable my child to be able to accept him or herself.

24. Be adaptable. I will expose my child to different situations so that he or she will be flexible enough to deal with the various stresses that will come life's way.

25. Be emotionally healthy. I will allow my child the ability to express him or herself in an accepting environment. I will also seek help for my child if he or she shows prolonged symptoms of emotional trouble.

26. Be fun. I will teach my child how to have fun and how to laugh.
27. Be focused. Help children develop clear goals for themselves, both short term and long term.

Authority Is Essential

28. Being firm with your child is NOT the same as being mean.

29. Your child will respect you more if you believe you are supposed to be the authority in the relationship.

30. The 60s generation lost the concept that authority is a good thing. Authority is essential to maintaining order and structure in a family.

31. Establishing authority (in a kind way) with a child enhances creativity. The boundaries are known and the child does not have to continually test them, leaving energy for more productive activities.

32. Establishing authority (in a kind way) with a child will help them deal with authority as an adult.

33. Mean what you say. Don't allow guilt to cause you to back down on what you know is right.

Your Relationship With Your Child Is The Key To Success

34. Your personal relationship with your child matters to their emotional well being! Many parents underestimate their influence over a child. With a good relationship, the child will come to you when they need to. When there is a bad relationship, the child will seek out others (such as peers) for counsel.

35. With a good parent-child relationship almost any form of discipline will work. With a poor parent-child relationship almost any form of discipline won't work.

36. Respect your child. Treat them at home as you would in front of others. This also teaches children to be authentic with others.

37. Spend some "special time" with your child each day, doing what they want to do. 15 to 20 minutes a day of "special time" will strengthen the bond between you and your child and make a dramatic difference in the quality of your relationship. Being available to the child will help him or her feel important and enhance his or her self esteem.

38. Be a good listener. Find out what the child thinks before you tell him or her what you think.

39. Get down on their level when you talk with a child.

40. Speak softly to children. They're much more likely to hear you.

41. Avoid yelling at children. How do you feel when someone yells at you? When someone yells at me I cannot hear what they are saying and I get mad. Children are no different.

42. Keep promises to children.

43. Children learn about relationships from watching how their parents relate to each other. Are you setting a good example?

A Loving, Helpful Environment

44. Tell a child you love him or her everyday.

45. Touch a child everyday.

46. Establish eye contact with a child everyday and inquire about their day.

47. Take the time to hug a child whenever they climb into your lap (or into your space).

48. Listen to their music to hear what information is being fed into their mind.

49. Limit TV and video games. These are often "no-brain" activities and of little help for children.

50. Don't allow kids to watch too much of the news. It'll scare them and increase their internal sense of anxiety.

51. Rituals (bed time, meal time, holidays, etc.) provide continuity, structure, and stability for children.
52. Introduce children to a multitude of experiences, even if they are hesitant.

53. Play games with your kids. Recreation is essential to a balanced, happy life.

Clear Expectations

54. Be clear with what you expect with a child or teen. It is effective for families to have posted rules, spelling out the "laws" and values of the family. Here are 8 examples:

1. TELL THE TRUTH

2. TREAT EACH OTHER WITH RESPECT

3. NO ARGUING WITH PARENTS

4. RESPECT EACH OTHER'S PROPERTY

5. DO WHAT MOM AND DAD SAY THE FIRST TIME
   (without complaining or throwing a fit)

6. ASK PERMISSION BEFORE YOU GO ANYWHERE

7. PUT THINGS AWAY THAT YOU TAKE OUT

8. LOOK FOR WAYS TO BE KIND AND HELPFUL TO EACH OTHER

Notice What You Like A Lot More Than What You Don't Like

55. When a child lives up to the rules and expectations, be sure to notice him or her. If you never reinforce good behavior you're unlikely to get much of it.

56. Notice the behaviors you like in your child 10 times more than the behaviors you don't like. This teaches them to notice what they like about themselves rather than to grow up with a critical self-image.

57. Praise and encouragement enhance good behavior and teach children new skills. Anger and punishment suppress difficult behavior but do not teach children anything good in the long run.

58. Praise and encouragement strengthens the parent-child bond. Anger erodes the parent-child bond.

Discipline

59. Do not tell a child to do something 10 times. Expect a child to comply the first time! Be ready to back up your words.

60. Never discipline a child when you're out of control. Take a time out before you lose your cool.

61. Use discipline to teach a child rather than to punish or get even for bad behavior.

62. See misbehavior as a problem you're going to solve rather than "the child is just trying to make you mad."

63. It's important to have swift, clear consequences for broken rules, enforced in a "matter of fact" and unemotional way. Nagging and yelling are extremely destructive and ineffective.

64. In parenting, always remember the words "firm and kind." One parent used the phrase, "tough as nails and kind as a lamb." Try to balance them at the same time.

65. When the child is stuck in negative behavior, try to distract them and come back to the issue later.

66. Deal with lying and stealing immediately.

67. Do not back away from dealing with difficult situations with your teenagers (sex, drugs, disrespect). Deal with them in a kind, firm way!

68. Many parents ask me about whether or not spanking a child is helpful. I tell them that spanking is never the issue. The issue is the quality of your relationship with the child and your ability to be firm and kind with them. With a good relationship between a parent and a child almost any form of discipline seems to work. When the parents and child have a poor relationship most forms of discipline do not work.

Choices

69. Give a child choices between alternatives, rather than dictating what they'll do, eat or wear. If you make all the decisions for your child he or she will be unable to make their own decisions later on.

70. Before you tell a child what you think about a decision in his life, ask him to tell you what's on his mind.

71. Encourage a child to make independent decisions, based on the knowledge he or she has, rather than on what friends might say or do.

Supervision

72. Supervise a child's school experience. Get to know the teacher. Be an active part of the class. Sometimes parents are the last people to know things are going wrong. Being involved will help keep your child on track.

73. Know where your child or teen is at all times. Tell your child that you want to know who they are with, what they are doing and what time they'll be home. Let him or her know that you are going to periodically check. Initially they'll complain about your intrusion, but in the long run they will appreciate your caring and concern.

74. Trust is based on past experience. Let your children know that their level of freedom is based on how trustworthy they show themselves to be.

75. Spend time with your child's friends (even if they turn you off), to know the kind of influence that your child is exposed to.

Parental Support

76. Parents need to be together and support each other.

77. When children are allowed to split parental authority they have far more power than is good for them.

78. Parents need time for themselves. Parents who are drained do not have much left that is good for their children.

79. The best thing you can do for your children is to love your spouse.

Self-Esteem

80. Children live up to the labels we give them. Be careful of the nicknames and phrases you use to describe your children.

81. A child's self-esteem is more important than the quality of his or her homework.

82. Help children to have islands of competence in areas of interest to them (sports, music, etc.). Self-esteem is often based on a person's ability to feel competent.

Teaching Children

83. A significant way in which children learn values is by watching the behavior of their parents. Teach children values with your behavior.

84. Teach children from your own real life experiences.

85. Teach your children about sex and drugs. Don't leave the responsibility up to the school! Things are different now then when you and I were growing up.

86. Help children learn from their mistakes. Don't berate or belittle them, otherwise they will do that to themselves when they're less than perfect.

87. Have only good food in the house to eat, so that children will learn how to eat in ways that'll help them be healthy.

88. Exercise with a child. Help them make exercise a routine in their lives.

89. Teach children about a kind, caring, loving, forgiving God.

90. Teach children that there is a beginning and an end to life.

91. Teach children to predict the best things for themselves.

92. Don't allow a child to blame others for how his or her life is turning out.
93. Teach children the power of delegation.

94. Teach children to send Thank You notes.

95. Teach your child organization skills to make their life easier. (This may mean making them keep the bedroom organized, even when he or she may not be naturally inclined that way.)

96. Read to children (or have them read to you) often.

97. Teach kids to type.

98. Teach children new technology (computers, etc.)

Work and Children

99. Don't give them everything they ask for. Encourage them to work for what they want.

100. Work is good for children, doing everything for them is not.

Siblings

101. Encourage and reward respect among siblings. Discipline inappropriate or hostile behavior between siblings.

102. Some sibling rivalry is normal. Remember the story of the first siblings in the Bible. It didn't turn out so well.

Friends and Peers

103. Don't fight a child's battle with their friends or peers, but be available as a consultant.

When There Are Problems

104. Seek help for your child when there are problems. Don't sweep them under the rug. Teach kids to talk about the things that aren't working in their lives.

105. Apologize to children when you make a mistake.

106. Help children see past their disabilities and weaknesses.

Understand What's Normal

107. Understand normal development (e.g., the terrible twos, independence and identity in teens).

108. When a teenager pulls away from you, pursue him or her with kindness not anger.

109. Don't tell an 18 year old what to do. They are likely to do the opposite. Suggest alternatives, listen, help with options. Be careful with your words. They're likely to be how I was and say something like "I'm 18. I can do whatever I want."

Learn All You Can

110. Effective parenting is a learned skill. Work to learn all you can.

Brain Interventions

111. Make children wear helmets when riding a bike, skateboarding, rollerblading and in high-risk situations

112. Make children wear seatbelts all the time

113. Balanced diets with less refined sugars and carbohydrates

114. Teach them how to think positive healthy thoughts and raise healthy internal anteaters to rid themselves of ANTs (automatic negative thoughts)

115. Everyday, have them focus on the things they are grateful for in their life

116. Have them watch the Disney movie Pollyanna, at least yearly

117. Surround them with great smells

118. Have them build a library of wonderful experiences

119. Regularly exercise with them

120. Teach them diaphragmatic breathing

121. Teach children how to effectively confront and deal with conflictual situations

122. Have them develop clear goals for their life (relationships, school, work, money, and self) and look at them everyday.

123. Focus on what you like about their behavior a lot more than what you don't like

124. Make naturally oppositional children mind you the first time (through a firm, kind, authoritative stance)

125. Sing and hum with your children whenever you can

126. Make beautiful music a part of their lives

127. Touch them often (appropriately)

128. Dance and music lessons need to be part of their lives

129. Take head injuries seriously, even minor ones

130. Take medications when needed

131. Eliminate most caffeine

132. Do not use much alcohol around children and never use any illegal drugs around children

133. Have children avoid contact sports where head injuries are common, do not let them hit soccer balls with their heads

134. Do not let children bang their head when frustrated

135. Do not let children spend time with people who do drugs, fight, or are involved in other dangerous activities

CLEAR GOALS FOR PARENTS AND KIDS

POSITIVE RELATIONSHIP
(time and a willingness to listen)

CLEAR EXPECTATIONS

POSITIVE REINFORCEMENT

CLEAR, UNEMOTIONAL CONSEQUENCES

SUPERVISION

CHOICES

About Dr. Amen

Daniel Amen, M.D. is a clinical neuroscientist, child and adult psychiatrist and the medical director of the Amen Clinic in Fairfield, California. The recipient of numerous writing and research awards, Dr. Amen's pioneering brain imaging research has been featured around the world. He is a nationally recognized expert in the fields of "the brain and behavior," parent training and attention deficit disorder. He is the author of several books, including *Change Your Brain, Change Your Life, Windows into the ADD Mind* and *Firestorms in the Brain.*

About The Amen Clinic

The Amen Clinic for Behavioral Medicine is a private medical clinic which specializes in innovative diagnosis and treatment for a wide variety of neuropsychiatric, behavioral and learning problems for children, teenagers and adults. Established in 1989 by Daniel G. Amen, M.D., the center has a national reputation for evaluating and treating Attention Deficit Disorder (ADD) and related problems. Other psychiatric disorders such as depression, obsessive-compulsive disorders, anxiety, aggressiveness, school failure, marital conflicts and parent-child problems are also evaluated and treated. The Amen Clinic is well known for its innovative work with brain SPECT imaging.

350 Chadbourne Road
Fairfield, CA 94585
phone (707) 429-7181
fax (707) 429-8210
web site: www.amenclinic.com and brainplace.com